# THE ONLY AUTHENTIC BOOK OF PERSUASION:

*The Agenda–Spin Method 8th Edition*

## RICHARD E. VATZ
*Towson University*

*Library of Congress Control Number* 2025904484

978-1-965552-18-6 (Paperback)

BOOKWRIGHTS
HOUSE

admin@bookwrightshouse.com
☎ (213) 286 6700

To MY LATE, NEARLY perfect parents Allen and Ginny Vatz, my inestimable family including my wife Joanne, my daughter Shaina, son-in-law Walter and son David, as well as through 2022 my brother Ken and my closest friend Lee Weinberg and my best students of 50 years David Schwartz, the late Mark Loechel and Bill Owens, Executive Editor of "60 Minutes," all wonderful and erudite family and friends who have persuaded me at times to change my erring thoughts or ways, once-in-a-while successfully. To Kiri Bea, my saintly granddaughter, and her incredible brother, Abraham Stephen, who both promise to surpass all of their older kin in all their great qualities, if possible. To former Maryland Governor Robert L. Ehrlich, who has singularly guest-spoken to my Persuasion class twice a year for over twenty-five years and is personally the most impressive political actor I have ever known or read about.

I should also like to thank those in academia most responsible for my rhetorical development: the late Dr. Thomas Szasz, the late literally unsurpassable University of Pittsburgh Professor Emeritus Trevor Melia, Dr. Robert P. Newman, Dr. Jack Fruchtman, Dr. George Hahn, Dr. Teodora Carabas Salow, my close friend, the late Dr. Ron Rabin, and up until he stopped talking to anyone who voted for Donald Trump, my great writing partner Dr. Jeffrey Schaler. I want to give a particularly hearty thank-you to the finest and most responsible editor with whom I have ever worked, Professor John Ware, former Chair of the Department of Fine Arts at Virginia Union University and members of TRWC. I also want to thank a great friend, sports writer and professor, Mark Hyman, who has provided me with undilutedly good judgment in our many conversations about persuasion, particularly as it pertains to academic politics. Also, I would like to dedicate this book to the vast majority of students and faculty and a number of administrators, especially my long-term chairman, the late Charles Flippin, my uniquely-great, high-integrity colleague, Jennifer Potter, my exceptional former chair Diane Wood, and my remarkably splendid dean, Dr. Laurie Mullen, and her uniquely outstanding staff and the College of Education (COE), and my great Towson president, the late Maravene Loeschke and her only equal, president Mark Ginsberg and his best staff I have ever seen at a college or university, all of whom I have known at Towson University over the years who understand that good persuasion entails neither anger nor feeling threatened by a good argument, nor giving in when you are in the right.

The presidential and COE staffs, may I repeat, are incredible, just incredible.

I also would like to thank my 60-year membership in the National Communication Association whose governance ended up by 2025 with these who still support freedom of speech even in fractious times: David McMahan, Ray McKerrow, Bill Balthrop, and Carole Blair.

More striking in their support of speech freedom and help supporting this book are found in the leadership of the Eastern Communication Association's Jeanne Persuit, Jennifer Waldeck, Stacy Smulowitz, Jordan Atkinson, Jessica Papajcik, Leeanne M. Bell McManus, Katherine Thweatt, Cheryl Casey and Kathie Cesa for sponsoring and guiding me quickly to establish the Eastern Communication Association's "Richard E. Vatz Agenda-Spin Persuasion Award," great friends and colleagues D.L. Stephenson, Theodore Sheckels, J. Kanan Sawyer, Barb K. Kaye and John M. Ware for generously serving on the Committee for the Award. I also want to thank Duquesne's brave Eric Grabowski for his courageous consequential political support in the stultifying liberal climes of the academy.

And finally, I should like to thank Speaker Nancy Pelosi for speaking to my Persuasion class on October 4, 2018, which demonstrates that people of significantly different political views can act with comity in this very polarized country. She was wonderful.

https://www.towson.edu/news/2018/pelosivisit.html?utm_source=news&utm

# Contents

EVER SINCE I WAS a child, I have been fascinated by persuasion. When I was growing up, I used to wonder how certain topics found their way to my home dinner table. I saw my dad and brother in lengthy conversations, battling it out for interpretation of the issues they had somehow decided to address. This was almost a nightly wonderment, excerpt for the dinners following events at which my brother or I was bullied by the local violent miscreant. On those few occasions the minor battles were discussed. There was no decision to be made on what topic would be addressed by our family at those times. Bullying physically imposed itself on us. There are few matters in life that are literally unavoidable as persuasive topics. When Hiroshima and Nagasaki were bombed with atomic weapons, for much of the world there was nothing to be discussed instead of those unsurpassable events.

As I progressed through my youth, my near-obsession with persuasion never abated. I took it as a course in college, and I went into the field of rhetoric and communication for my master's and doctorate. Rhetoric was defined by Aristotle as "discovery of the available means of persuasion," which topic and definition captivated me due to my life-long fascination and curiosity surrounding the identical, it seemed and seems to me, topic of persuasion. Still, that definition gnawed at me for a couple of reasons. One: if rhetoric is about persuasion's discovery, how does that make it different from persuasion itself? Two: I thought of the concept of persuasion as something that was created, not discovered. In fact, to argue that it was *discovered* seemed to me even then to pander to the passivity of human beings, a passivity that I thought typical of the perspective of too much of academic study: things *happened* to people: people don't *create* their happening.

More specifically, it seemed to me that if the study of persuasion—again synonymous with the study of rhetoric, my possible occupational field of professordom—merely accounted for investigating how persuasion worked in given *situations*, the field of rhetoric would become ancillary to other major fields of study, such as political science, whose credentials for analyzing persuasion far exceeded rhetoric's. Moreover, every field would be superior in analyzing its own persuasion again, political science for political persuasion; family studies for family persuasion; business administration for persuasion in business; and so on.

My first year of graduate school at the University of Pittsburgh was even more influential for me than for most. I had two professors who profoundly influenced my intellectual development, and while there were others, these two mattered the most. I had had them both as an undergraduate: Dr. Robert P. Newman created in me a focus on evidence, and he was—not coincidentally—the head of forensics at the University of Pittsburgh. My outlook on public debate was most affected by an incident—yes, an incident. There was a faculty disagreement involving Ray Lynn Anderson, young (late 20s) professor of rhetoric.

The disagreement concerned a faculty argument on the 11th Floor (if I recall correctly) of the Cathedral of Learning of Pitt. The professors were leveling rhetorical shots aimed at one another.

But Professor Anderson kept repeating the same phrase: "What is the issue?" If he said it once, he said it five to ten times.

No one could get a focus on that about which they were arguing.

I'm sure if I could reproduce the drama, some would argue that the answer was obvious; but it wasn't.

It has always been my style to decide that on which to focus and then try to infuse it with the meaning or spin I wished to create, thus completing the theoretical framework for my lifelong battle with those who think that situations—whatever they are—determine persuasion and rhetoric which follow from the situations.

When I wrote the well-known-in-my-field article "The Myth of the Rhetorical Situation," I must have had that verbal battle in my graduate department of the late 1960s in mind.

The first question in all persuasion is "What is the issue?" from which we move to what it means.

Then, around 1971, my best graduate college professor, Dr. Trevor Melia, introduced me to a major article in my field, Lloyd Bitzer's "The Rhetorical Situation," published in the very first issue of rhetoric's preeminent journal, *Philosophy and Rhetoric*. I read through the article, absolutely captivated by what I regarded as its irresponsible theoretical take on persuasion. Virtually every line in the piece actually offended me, as it argued that persuasion and rhetoric were the passive, relatively unimportant studies that I feared so many people thought. The article's last paragraph stated, "In the best of all possible worlds, there would be communication perhaps, but no rhetoric—since exigences would not arise," and ended by saying that "persuasion…lacks philosophical warrant as a practical discipline."

There I had my "eureka" moment. Not only were all of my intuitive instincts confirmed by this heralded (and still celebrated) definition of rhetoric and persuasion, but every suspicion I had concerning the probably permanent second-class status of the field of rhetoric was also corroborated.

I went to work on my own article, refuting on paper each line that I believed was not only wrong-headed, but also field destructive. Every argument seemed to come naturally, although I was always aware of the slogan that when you have only a hammer, everything appears to be a nail.

I have been a conservative all of my life, although I was a social liberal during the days of Martin Luther King's civil rights movement. I spent my first two collegiate years at Vanderbilt University when that school had just become integrated, and my commitment to the concept of equal opportunity was always with me. Still, the enterprise of persuasion and rhetoric (remember, synonymous terms in this book) always seemed to be to be politically neutral. Yet, I noticed that virtually every use of rhetoric and its derivatives in the original "rhetorical situation" piece as well as subsequent applications of it seemed to serve liberal ideology. Literally all of Bitzer's examples did.

I finished my article on persuasion, countering "The Rhetorical Situation," and I titled it "The Myth of the Rhetorical Situation." I sent it to the editor of Philosophy and Rhetoric, rhetorical icon Carroll Arnold, and in two weeks he sent me an acceptance, asking for two changes: (1) a new name for the piece (I don't recall the specifics of the suggestion) and (2) excising a paragraph in which I had discussed the paradox that my "Myth" piece itself entailed struggles for salience and meaning (later to be added: agenda and spin—see "Mythical Status" chapter below) and that its precepts could also analytically be applied to "The Rhetorical Situation" article.

I politely begged Dr. Arnold not to change the title, but I acceded on the excision request. I had long been enthralled with Dr. Thomas Szasz's *The Myth of Mental Illness*, and I had already become a bit of an acolyte to him; a role, parenthetically, that grew and became a friendship over the years. I believed that my perspective on persuasion was quite consistent with his writings on mental illness, and it was tremendously satisfying to me to have an article titled similarly to his *magnum opus*.

Three articles, "The Myth of the Rhetorical Situation," a follow-up piece that was the lead article in The Review of Communication, January 2009, elucidating the place of the piece in understanding persuasion, "The Mythical Status of Situational Rhetoric: Implications for Rhetorical Critics' Relevance in the Public Arena;" and an article on an assignment I have given to every persuasion class I have taught in my over 40 straight years of teaching that course, "The Article Rewrite Assignment" in the 2006 volume of The Successful Professor, constitute three chapters in this volume.

Two powerful motives move my support of the salience-agenda/meaning-spin model, now changed for simplicity to the Agenda/Spin model, that constitutes my perspective on persuasion. In my nearly four decades years of collegiate teaching, during which I have won more teaching awards than anyone else on my campus, I have seen students utterly fascinated by this perspective. My great colleague, Professor of English H. George Hahn, once wrote a letter supporting me for an award and ironically referred to my persuasion class as having "mythical" status in its campus popularity. In all of those years I have never had less than overwhelmingly positive student evaluations of the course. It is all owing to this exciting perspective on rhetoric, which makes the *field* of rhetoric a primary one.

The second motive has been my disdain-and forgive me, colleagues, and readers, my contempt for most current persuasion texts. I have never used one of those books as a primary work in my classes. The exceptions are two books by *The New York Times* bestselling author, Harrison Monarth: *Executive Presence: The Art of Commanding Respect Like a CEO* and *Breakthrough Communication,* which, especially the latter, explicate the philosophies articulated in this book. All of the major texts focusing on persuasion, however-all of them-are reflective of the situational philosophy, and most include emphases on formal and informal logic (irrelevant to persuasion as defined herein), empirical studies (almost all of which are anathema to understanding persuasion and utterly worthless, save for seeming to authenticate a field of study), invalid psychological analysis of persuasion (e.g., attitude studies, cognitive dissonance, subliminal persuasion) and/or incorrectly emphasized analysis of the ethics of persuasion. On this last matter, almost all ethical analyses of persuasion are general, and yet impossible to apply generally. Standard concepts of right and wrong-fairness of generalization, authenticity, and the like-apply, but they are mostly matters not requiring expertise in *persuasion.* It is not helpful, it is argued here, to provide a checklist of ethical values or do's and don'ts, but the one ethical injunction that pervades this work is the assumption of responsibility: persuaders are morally responsible for that which they try to make salient (or make part of the agenda) as well as their choices of the meanings (or spin) they try to infuse for chosen audiences.

Let me just focus on a couple of representative standard texts. One, parenthetically mostly written by a senior author whom I admired as I went through graduate school because he The Agenda-Spin Model of my major mentor, is particularly without merit. Full disclosure demands that I inform you, hardened reader, that I have a profound personal disaffection which has built up in recent years for this writer, a disaffection I believe that has not caused my animosity to his work; but you be the judge.

He is a political liberal who for many conventions was singularly assigned by the National Communication Association (NCA) to set up panels that would examine ideological disputes within and without the field and profession.

In most years (and perhaps all years), he set up panels that were disproportionately liberal (one year, 7 to 1 by my count), and in some of these sessions he had secured literally zero conservatives from the NCA to be participants. Moreover, when criticized for his ideological discrimination, this well-known, urbane professor was unwilling to discuss the problem and became angry, losing his clever urbanity in the process. Lots of academics claim to believe in the "marketplace of ideas" but are uninterested in actually supporting open debate and discussion when the academic *zeitgeist* is challenged. To the credit of the NCA, newly run by presidents sensitive to the long-term discrimination against conservatives by the profession, he was eased out of this responsibility, although it took several years.

But I digress. In any case, his standard persuasion text, which I shall neither name nor publicize, is, as are most such texts, an amalgam of unfocused examinations of ethics, advertising examples, or what the authors call "paradigm cases," and psychology, yet nothing in this lengthy text (most persuasion texts are overly lengthy-that misleadingly communicates seriousness) really tells the reader exactly how persuasion works. There is a definition, defining persuasion as "human communication designed to influence the judgments and actions of others," but no meaningful single core center as to how persuasion is *effected.*

This text uses what so many use: the "kitchen sink" approach, by which everything that interests the authors is thrown in so that everyone can find something relevant to his or her concerns. In most chapters the discerning reader asks himself or herself, "What in the world does this have to do with persuasion?" Unfortunately, however, no reader will be able to persuade any better, because of the book's neglect to use the examples to demonstrate *precisely how to persuade others.*

Another text, written no doubt by a nicer and more professional professor, if not a more industrious one, is published by a major publisher and attempts to define persuasion precisely as "a symbolic process in which communicators try to persuade other people to change their attitudes or behaviors regarding an issue through the transmission of a message in an atmosphere of free choice" and then gives additional seemingly random "components."

This latter book, written as well with the always-present "kitchen sink" theory in mind, also taps psychological theories, touches on brainwashing and coercion-persuasion the author of this text doesn't much respect or find valid-focuses on campaigns and myths of persuasion that leave the reader predictably bored out of his or her mind once the test is taken to see how much students retain before forgetting all of it.

In addition, this work, less erudite than the one looked at above but similar in student response, exemplifies impenetrable academic prose likely sold back by nearly 100 percent of its student purchasers. Try this test: ask some student who has taken a persuasion course with one of the above tomes or a similar one what he or she specifically recalls about how to persuade people.

By contrast, nearly every week some former student tells me how he or she has used the lessons from my persuasion class in business, at home, and/or to understand how others attempt to persuade him or her. They use the framework in this book for their everyday lives, as ex-students have done for decades. And all these books have sections on logical fallacies…why? What do such fallacies have to do with persuasion? Adolph Hitler was a successfully persuasive leader of the most criminal regime in history, and if you read his Mein Kampf, virtually every line is illogical, but he persuaded the masses in his country. On the other hand, William F. Buckley, George F. Will, and E. J. Dionne were and are the writers with nary a logical flaw, and at least 95% of the American population is and was completely unpersuaded by them, either because they don't know them, don't understand them or disagree with them. Now, they are persuasive with their friends and family; but even there, George Will was divorced, and Buckley's son Christopher Buckley wrote a biography of his parents and apparently often found them not overly persuasive at times.

Logical fallacy analysis is filled with logical fallacies; name calling is "name calling;" citing an argument as a hasty generalization is often a hasty generalization; and *ad hominem* arguments may violate warnings about using fallacies, but they are sometimes quite effective in persuasion.

My definition of persuasion is as follows: Persuasion is the struggle for chosen agenda and the subsequent effort to infuse spin strategically into the established topic(s) for chosen audiences. The credibility of the source will affect (I so hate the verb "impact") the success of all persuasive endeavors. Source credibility (i.e., is this the source we shall allow to determine to what we pay attention and what its significance is?) is tremendously affected by mystification, or the bringing of awe to the struggle for agenda and spin.

Mystification enhances such credibility through age, position, numbers of persuaders, the appearance of knowledge lacked by the persuadee, and a number of other *ad hoc* factors: A parent is mystifying to a child; a doctor is usually mystifying to a patient; a group may be mystifying to an individual; and analyses utilizing science or apparent science can be particularly mystifying to credulous, uninformed audiences. The only time when there is no choice regarding establishment of agenda or spin is when an issue unavoidably affects people. Punch a bully in the mouth and see if you can get him to discuss astrophysics or interpret the punch as good natured.

This might be the propitious spot to make a claim or quasi-disclaimer. I am well known in my field for being conservative, although I am not a Republican. Nothing in the theory of persuasion propounded in this book applies *per se* more to liberal than to conservative politics. Persuasive analysis of all political points of view can apply the Agenda/Spin model. One of the clearest examples of successful rhetoric or persuasion in years was Bill O'Reilly's self-ennobling 'No-Spin Zone,' by which he claimed (before his show's 2017 cancellation by Fox) that he avoided rhetoric and persuasion both in the TV show and in his book. Bill, whose views I more often than not, but certainly not always, share, is an inveterate persuader, choosing what topics to cover, what facts to highlight, what facts to ignore and what meaning and spin with which to infuse it all.

The point is that there is no "No Spin Zone"—for anyone.

Another fascinating misleading example of conservative persuasion is to contrast the pictures of Michael Dukakis and Margaret Thatcher sitting in tanks. I submit that to argue, as virtually every human being in America eventually did in 1988, that Gov. Dukakis looks ridiculous in that picture, but that (my hero) Prime Minister Thatcher looks brave and resolute visiting troops in Fallingbostel, West Germany, is a triumph of rhetorical creation. They look about the same, although Thatcher's goggles perhaps look even more ridiculous.

If I could add to the endless definitions of what a "human" is, I would say it is he or she who chooses an issue or issues for an audience and tries to convince that audience that the issue(s) mean x, y or z but not a, b or c.

Man is the persuading animal.

# Chapter 1

# THE AGENDA/SPIN MODEL OF PERSUASION EXPLAINED

❖

FOR OVER 45 YEARS there has been an academic fight on the relationship between rhetoric and situations. Lloyd Bitzer, author of the 1968 article, "The Rhetorical Situation," offers a perspective that virtually makes rhetoric an important study. This "situational perspective," as I label it, argues that reality presents us with an agenda with inherent meaning and significance. The rhetoric surrounding the situation—the language and symbols describing it and making recommendations regarding what actions the situation "demands" (a favorite term of the situational side)—follows naturally and inexorably. The "rhetorical perspective," my concept as articulated in previous and subsequent chapters, argues with persuaders' struggle with one another—as individuals, as group members, as loosely associated collaborators—to decide what constitutes the situation with which we are dealing. This entails two components aimed at chosen audiences: the first is creating salience and creating agendas for chosen audiences or simply determining what we talk about. The second component constitutes persuaders' creating meaning and/or spin for the chosen agenda.

Rhetoric and persuasion—yet again, synonymous terms—are ubiquitous. Virtually every communication is an effort to create issue salience or attention of the chosen audience, and with every such effort there is a simultaneous effort to characterize the salience or agenda item(s) with specified meaning or interpretation. This effort usually also involves focus on a chosen piece or pieces of evidence and the ignoring or diminishing of other pieces of evidence, all part of the rhetorical process.

## Persuasion in Different Environments

In addition to the defining factors just cited, there is what I would term a new and permanent anarchy of persuasion which has begun seriously in the current century. The business of the competition to create agenda and to infuse it with spin is open, if not equally open, to virtually everyone today. Through blogs, Facebook, Twitter, and other special media there is a hyper-fragmented competition among those individuals and small groups to create agenda and spin for selected audiences.

The economic consequences of this fragmentation of persuasion competition are impossible to handicap, but are manifestly devastating for newspapers, television news, and other news outlets, whatever the benefits might be for other segments of society. The social consequences are beyond the scope of this book, but are inestimable for reasons including the inability to eradicate many persuasive communications from the Internet, as once material is online and captured by search engines, it cannot ever be removed from the public sphere with certainty. Pay attention, students, who don't realize that sexting in 2000s may haunt you through the 21st Century.

There is an ongoing *intrapersonal* persuasion decision-making for most people: what to think about and what it means. Most individuals skip from topic to topic and meaning to meaning within themselves as simultaneous persuader and audience. For most folks there is little resistance, as most of us are quite friendly to ourselves as we make choices of what to think about and what meaning to assign to our personal choices of topics.

Do you think about work? Health? Your relationship with specific others? Sex? Several or all of these things? It is your choice as simultaneous speaker and audience. The term obsessed simply refers to people who make what the persuader estimates as untoward choices regarding personal agendas and spin.

On an *interpersonal* level, when one awakens in the morning and brings up a matter with an interlocutor, he or she is trying to set the agenda with that particular audience or auditor. When one retires at night, he or she may be an audience of a medium—radio, television, the Internet, Twitter—wherein a persuader is trying to establish an agenda with him or her and infuse meaning into chosen matters or issues.

During the day, meals with friends involve chosen audiences and messages initiated and accepted or rejected along with meanings and spins accepted or rejected. Often the success of the persuasion is a function of the *ethos* or standing of the persuader vis à vis the target audience(s) of the persuasion. If one cannot affect the topic(s) of conversation, much less their interruption, one is not very significant as a persuader and has insufficient perceived authority with his or her audience.

Two critical notes on the *ethos* of the persuader should be emphasized in this analysis, and one is the tremendous power of "reluctant testimony" in creating agenda and spin. Reluctant testimony is the claim that one is either making a point or interpreting a point contrary to one's own interests. Examples are everywhere, including conservative columnists/persuaders who supported, say, former Representative Andrew Weiner's (D-NY) right to finish out his term in the face of the sex scandal, to liberal academicians who fight for the tenure of conservative colleagues. The rhetorical danger in assuming rhetoric is "reluctant" is that hidden motives may be involved, removing the ostensible sincerity of persuading despite one's vested interest.

A second phenomenon peculiar to the study of rhetoric as outlined in this book is the "self-fulfilling prophecy." When a person accords himself or herself authority to interpret reality accurately, he or she can often affect somewhat the outcome of matters. Sometimes this is simple *confidence*, as when an athlete believes (intrapersonal persuasion) he can accomplish something as opposed to losing confidence and having, say, his tennis stroke affected. Self-fulfilling prophecy, however, can be applied broadly, as when a political principal says publicly that she "doesn't believe" she "can win the West Side vote," and fewer of her supporters come out to vote for her as a result of her prediction. Self-fulfilling prophecies, are, of course, self-persuasion wherein the very fact of an individual or group's predicting an event or anticipating an outcome creates or affects the outcome itself. In my Persuasion course we recently discussed the phenomenon of young people who are labeled "learning-disabled" and enter into the bureaucracy of self-diagnosis, special school dispensations (more time for tests, etc.) and interacting with other such labeled individuals. They become socialized to believe they cannot compete on an equal basis and then often by that socialization can not and do not compete on an equal basis.

The perpetrators of a self-fulfilling a prophecy may require a credulous audience. When a teacher of a pre-teen tells him or her that he or she "will never amount to anything," it constitutes an effective, but ethically bereft, communication.

Of course, one's effectiveness as a persuader will vary with the audience. A parent may have no competition with his or her child in determining what will be discussed, although there will be varying degrees of determining what the meaning of the accepted topic will be. With husband and wife, boyfriend and girlfriend, friends and lovers, there is a hierarchical determination of who may create agenda and spin. This hierarchy may change according to different sociological settings: when with the family, a son or daughter might have less power over the agenda and meanings than he or she has with just a sibling.

There are hierarchies in the workplace as well. A professor has almost *carte blanche* to determine topics and meanings of conversations in many social science and humanities classes, as does a parent with his or her child. In my classes I will typically begin a discussion on rhetoric by saying, "O.K. class, our first topic of conversation today will be Katy Perry." What does this substantively have to do with the course's topic? Who knows, but the instructor's perceived authority will more often than not be sufficient to determine the topic without the question, and I explain this to my class.

In my Media Criticism class one day, the organization of topics got so screwed up that it seemed almost nonsensical, and I thought that students would surely pick that up and complain. There is no way to tell whether they noticed it, but no one brought it up.

Similarly, there was no objection to the raising of Ms. Perry's name. Students begin writing or typing notes in their computer pages. We assume, in courses with more specifically determined areas of study, that the freedom to determine topics and meanings arbitrarily is a bit more restricted. In physics and, let's say, less mysteriously in Baseball 101, the opening reference to a pop singer would have quickly diminishing returns, but even there not immediately.

And, of course, with a stricter hierarchy between persuader and audience, say in a grade school setting, the instructor may indeed have absolute unlimited ability to establish the agenda and spin, as was the case in my grade school decades ago wherein the gym instructor spoke on trite life lessons for 35 of 40 minutes of each class. I won't specify his name here so as not to embarrass friends and relatives of the late Mr. Cyril Pitman.

When exercising rhetoric on an interpersonal basis, the seminal question is, "What shall we talk about?" Fred's marriage, taxes (city, state, and/or federal), Hollywood marriages and trysts, war in the Middle East, nuclear proliferation, and/or endless *et ceteras*? For each sociology there will be a struggle to determine what will be salient, what is the agenda, what it means, and what the persuasive spin will be. Audiences will comply or (less typically) object, if they perceive that they have standing to so do.

The courtroom, wherein traditionalists talk of "forensic rhetoric," is a setting where persuasion is omnipresent: what facts may be brought up; what witnesses may be called; what questions may be asked; what is the official and unofficial prestige of one of the primary persuaders, the judge? When you have rules, clear and unclear, in a persuasive setting, it is one more fascinating component to the salience-agenda/meaning-spin model.

## Different Sociologies of Persuasion

The other day I went to a funeral and heard a eulogy. Eulogies are purely rhetorical, with communicators highlighting and ignoring facts and assigning meaning and significance almost without any necessary reference to others' perceptions and certainly little necessary correspondence to some reality testing.

The deceased was a man of significant controversy during his working days, but not so according to the persuaders present at his funeral. To them he was a "hail fellow well met" individual, a generous, open chap, always willing to meet with those who had a problem with his organization's policies. He was a gentle man who would never criticize a colleague behind his back, and he never lost his temper.

To others not holding forth, who talked among themselves in quiet tones, the decedent was an utterly ineffectual leader who always pursued the lines of least resistance. He would consistently promise to resolve disputes but never did. He never followed up on complaints, but the supporters were, in a limited sense, quite correct: he indeed never refused to talk to anyone and was, despite its lack of a clear referent, a "nice guy."

No one lied in his or her public or private eulogistic remarks, but the different rhetorical depictions resembled the fabled story of blind men describing an elephant, which should be a classic rhetorical parable. Roughly, this perspective in John Godfrey Saxe's version involves six blind men who describe an elephant—depicting different parts as like a "spear," "snake," "tree," "fan," or "rope"—comprising different perspectives, but none untrue.

Again, *ethos*, or generally the credibility of the source, is particularly important respecting the ability to determine salience, agenda, meaning, and spin. If all given efforts to establish agenda and significance involve competition, part of that competition entails whether the persuader is perceived to have knowledge and fairness; more simply put, is the persuader a person or a source worth listening to, according to the intended audience?

Throughout a day, one encounters persuaders of more or less such standing. The child's main source for rhetorical creation of issues and meanings may be his or her parents. The parents' sources may be their friends, bosses, and/or media for some issues and may be community, state, or national or even international leaders speaking through media for others.

The range of sources, like rhetoric itself, is practically limitless. A student at the University of Texas at Tyler, Jordan Innerarity, working under Professor and Chair Dennis C. Cali, was assigned to assess whether successful persuasion implied the dominance of rhetoric or situations. His response struck the current author as quite insightful.

"Since we as humans have created rhetoric and symbols, we are the only things that can give an action or situation significance. I think these rhetorical situations are like paintings. You can paint a picture of a table and it is the picture that gives the table significance. The table itself didn't demand you to paint it. It was only the artist [who] decided that for some reason the table needed to be drawn. The same thing happens with rhetorical responses to situations. Only through my action of taking the time to talk about something do I give significance to the situation. I increase people's awareness with my words. If a situation had meaning on its own, we would have no need to speak about the situation. There would be universal understanding about the situation, but it doesn't work that way."

## Persuasion from a Rhetorical or Situational Perspective

For virtually every persuasive endeavor, the persuader portrays the suasory rhetoric as demanded by a correct reading of a situation which allegedly demands the attention and meaning that in fact he or she decides to assign to it. It is, paradoxically, more persuasive to imply that "reality dictates" attention and response (or lack of response) than to imply that the persuader is setting the agenda table himself or herself.

Let's look at political election persuasion. The "situational" side would say, for example, that the 2008 American presidential election was less about the Iraq war and more about the economy, because the war had wound down and the economy was tanking, and also that Senator John McCain had said that economics was not his strong suit. The "rhetorical side" would have said that the media ignored the successful "surge," and McCain did not bring it up until the third debate and not very strongly even then; McCain did not bring up—or did not successfully bring up—Obama's "evil companions" (Jeremiah Wright, William Ayers, Tony Rezko); McCain did not bring up that he was on the Senate Budget Committee and, therefore, due to these *rhetorical*, not situational, factors and others, the economy was established by Democratic persuaders as the number 1 issue, and it hurt McCain. Obama successfully deployed "change" as his term, but no sufficiently important persuader in the press or elsewhere successfully demanded that he say precisely what would be changed and how.

All politics is persuasive struggles involving salience-agenda and meaning-spin. During the 2012 Republican presidential primaries—and, of course, it must be restated that this struggle exists every day and every hour of political campaigns—there was not only such a persuasive fight between candidates, but between moderators and candidates.

CNN's John King, who in mid-June of 2011 hosted a Republican presidential debate http://redmaryland. blogspot.com/2011/06/republican-candiates-debate-in-new.html and consistently made derisive sounds to communicate his dissatisfaction with the answer and/or the length of the answer, hosted the January 19 debate (see lengthier account of these incidents in "Newt Gingrich vs. CNN's John King and Wolf Blitzer on Media Bias: Outcome, 1-1," Red Maryland, http://www.redmarylandblogspot.com www.redmarylandblogspot. com, January 29, 2012.). King started the South Carolina debate of January 19, 2012 by asking if Newt Gingrich would "like to take some time to respond" to an ABC interview in which his ex-wife said he asked her to "enter into an open marriage" at a time during which he was "having an affair." In a lengthy response Gingrich also ensured that there was a personal component of his outrage, saying in answer to King's claim that he did not initiate the issue: "John, John, it was repeated by your network. You chose to start the debate with it. Don't try to blame somebody else for bringing up such an irrelevant, personal issue."

This is classic persuasion in politics: King tried to insert an issue whose salience would be detrimental to Republicans, and one of those Republicans (Gingrich) tried to change the issue-at-hand by denigrating its choice, besmirching its author and asserting his own ethos to make something else the issue (media bias). King's compromised ethos as a media principal with left-wing bias was easy to attack persuasively.

The subject was changed successfully.

Persuasion is an art, of course, and when Gingrich tried to accuse Wolf Blitzer in a CNN January 26 debate of similar biases and agenda inappropriateness, he failed.

After the debate had gone on for some time, Blitzer asked Gingrich, "Earlier this week, you said Governor [Mitt] Romney, after he released his taxes, you said that you were satisfied with the level of transparency of his personal finances when it comes to this. And I just want to reiterate and ask you, are you satisfied right now with the level of transparency by the language of the attack?" Gingrich responded, "This is a nonsense question. Look, how about if the four of us agree for the rest of the evening, we'll actually talk about issues that relate to governing America?" Blitzer defended himself: "But, Mr. Speaker, you made an issue of this. This week, when you said that, 'He lives in a world of Swiss bank and Cayman Island bank accounts'. I didn't say that. You did." Gingrich argued that the question was illegitimate because it quoted him from "an interview on some TV show…" but that this was a "national debate." Gov. Romney asked rhetorically, "Wouldn't it be nice if people didn't make accusations somewhere else that they weren't willing to defend here?" Decision: Mr. Blitzer. Romney's ethos in combination with Blitzer's fair reputation overcame Gingrich's, and the issues became Gingrich's tax positions and rhetorical recklessness.

A parenthetical note to persuasion buffs: my problem is with Bitzer; I have no problem with Blitzer. At least I had no problem with the "pre-Resistance" Wolf Blitzer, who used to be one of the finest newspeople on the air.

The "Myth" pieces argue that rhetors are the keys to what is perceived as the dominant situation at hand, what parts (e.g. facts) are weighed as relevant, and what it all means (i.e., spin and framing).

What a student using the rhetorical perspective would ask is: Who determines what is perceived as the dominant situation, what determines what are seen as the relevant facts that deserve our attention, and how are language and symbols manipulated to make which audiences perceive that rhetorically-determined situation?

At base the agenda/spin model of persuasion illustrates that matter does not become issued for public consideration unless the following has occurred: a persuader or persuaders make a matter salient for chosen audiences, and those audiences put it on or have it put on their agenda for discussion and/or consideration. The matter thus is transformed into an "issue," and its perceived importance is a function of the persuader's success in making it part of a particular agenda.

Persuasion affects all people and all interests, and can be local, national, and/or international.

Issues and campaigns are wonderful examples for examination regarding the current model of persuasion at work. There may be no better an example of this than the rhetorical success of the current president, Donald Trump, to make alleged biased media—much of which he terms "the Fake Media" or "The *Very Fake Media*"—a continuing national issue. This is discussed in a later chapter, but the issue of the media being, as Trump has famously put it, including ABC, CBS, NBC, CNN, and *The New York Times* (the latter two having been excluded from a press briefing as of this writing), the "enemy of the American people" has been created by the President. This matter has been sustained in presidential communications, even wherein not at all anticipated, such as his Inaugural. The media have been strongly resented by conservative politicians for decades, perhaps beginning with Barry Goldwater in 1964, but it never became a dominant national issue until 2016 via Trump, and he has sustained it as well to the current day.

Similarly, when Barack Obama decided to make health care his signal issue the first year of his presidency, it was a *choice*, and his public diminishing of the matter of Iran's acquisition of a nuclear weapon was a rhetorical choice. He could easily have made other matters more important issues, and he could have put universal health care on the back burner.

President Obama tries to control the agenda for his run for re-election.

As president, Obama had the power or the perceived authority (*ethos*) to control much of the negative agenda, especially when he had a Democratic Congress, but to a particularly large degree when his political party controlled the Senate and the president holds the veto power. The Republicans tried in 2011 and 2012 to make the passed health care policy-which was labeled "Obamacare" by both supporters and critics-salient and part of political agenda. This appeared to be persuasively successful for the Republicans, but only when the rollout was problematic and when the reassurances that people could not lose their coverage or doctors, undisputed claims, were proved to be false.

## The Role of Reality

One objection to the rhetorical versus the situational dominance in persuasion is the feeling, perhaps intuition, that "reality" must have a role; one cannot simply act as if it doesn't exist.

I agree, to a limited extent.

There are specifiable, minimal constraints that reality creates relating to efforts to be persuasive with particular audiences.

Those who argue that the situation affects profoundly the rhetoric are not without an argument. You may argue, as I did in the opening chapter of this book, that those few situations that directly affect one's empirical reality may be unavoidable as a matter of rhetorical consideration. If one is at Ground Zero in New York City on September 11, 2001, one would not and could not successfully argue the choice component of rhetoric primarily. If one is bitten by a snake, his or her focusing on the pain and consequences of the bite is not seen as a representative effect of rhetor-controlled salience or agenda, even intrapersonally.

But even in such cases, a typical though they may be in understanding rhetoric, the interpretive component of rhetoric still has a tremendously important contribution from the perspective of control of the rhetor.

Say a person is in a flood. The unavoidable salience induced by the flood still leaves the interpretive component open to persuasive choices: Does the self-persuader infer helplessness? Should the government pay for his or her relief?

If one is under bombardment in a war theater and is facing bombs from several directions, no one could say that the salience of the bombs was created rhetorically, even though, again, the interpretation could vary per the rhetorical characterizations made by the individual interpersonally or intrapersonally.

Regardless, the great preponderance of public persuasion indeed involves portrayals of situations that are not interestingly constrained by a "real" situation. That which is made salient and part or all of the agenda involves choice: choice of what constitutes a or *the* "situation;" choice of what elements to include in the persuasion relating to the "situation," and the interpretation of the significance of the situation.

The second component of persuasion, interpretation or meaning/spin, is almost co-equal in importance to salience-agenda. I say "almost," because without a matter being put on the agenda for an audience, no one even *gets* to interpretation. A 9-year old hits his sister. A parent sees it without being detected; it may never be on the parents' agenda or even much on the child's agenda, unless the child who was hit mentions it and unless it is accepted as an issue. The parent decides to make the hit salient: "Hey, Jimmy, I saw you hitting Jennifer!"

Now the parent has carte blanche—due to the limited, quite young audience members—to interpret the hit. The parent could make a small deal of it: "Jimmy, play nice," with the implicit interpretation being that that behavior is unacceptable, but not actionable. The parent could make a big deal of it: "O.K., Jimmy, I saw that, and you're going to be spanked [or punished in some other way]."

How about illegal violence and its salience and interpretation? A drunk driver kills another. He's apprehended, tried, and convicted. The sentencing hearing will determine the interpretation of how egregious the killing was. Years ago claims of the perpetrator's "suffering from alcoholism" were somewhat or even fully exculpatory. But what facts are "relevant?" In forensic rhetoric there are rules of what evidence may be admitted, but this hardly changes the fact that some facts will be advanced while some will be omitted. As questioned earlier, who may testify? If, after conviction, there is a sentencing hearing, what and who are permitted at such a hearing to affect the agenda and interpretations? In recent years, testimony has been permitted in some venues illustrating the character of a victim and/or the effect of the crime on the victim's life and the lives of the victim's loved ones. In other venues in past years the family of deceased victims was not permitted to say anything.

On the level of national politics, the agenda/spin model is virtually the only game in town. Presidents are always trying to create an agenda and interpretation, and political competitors are always trying to change it. Political campaigns are perfect examples. Some incumbents try to focus on issues that are important to them, irrespective of their (the incumbents') generating or not generating support.

President Obama's first year in office could have centered on a variety of issues, including Iran's possible acquisition of nuclear weapons, the financial reform, problems in the Middle East, and others. As indicated above, he chose to focus on national health insurance, for reasons that are not relevant to rhetorical analysis. Regardless, there can be no argument made that there had been a situational change over the preceding year which made the president's new salience or new agenda item unavoidable. Do budgetary debates over the deficit and national debt require discussion of health care policy? I say yes. You say no. Can we mention an old Beatles tune here? Yes.

Analysis of agenda/spin creation does not require motivational analysis. This falls in the area of psychology, which is a rhetoric itself, as the author has written on extensively.

Applications of the agenda/spin creation model are as ubiquitous as persuasion itself. In my own corpus relating to persuasion I have written quite extensively on applications to politics, psychiatry, and public opinion. The first two are discussed at length here, but one of my first major uses of the model was regarding persuasion and public opinion ("Public Opinion and Presidential Ethos") and was published in *Western Speech and Communication* about 35 years ago. The piece dealt with how using public opinion polling, through establishing saliences and agenda and infusing selected matters with meaning and spin, was a type of persuasion. In other words, ostensibly *measuring* opinion was a way to *create* opinion. I have written on the persuasion of public opinion often, but not as often as I have written on political and psychiatric persuasion.

Here is but a sample from many such applications (and Chapter V will include further "exemplars"):

> For years, as I indicated above, sentencing hearings throughout American courtrooms have allowed for all of the exculpating and "understanding" rhetoric to be permitted to influence judges and juries to understand better why a convicted lawbreaker did what he or she did. In many venues there was no opportunity comparable to what exists now in many locales: victim impact statements. In a murder case, the disparity was particularly sad, as the deceased is obviously not present to win the sympathy of those sentencing, and family and relatives were often prevented from making statements. Some time ago The Washington Post reported on victim impact videos "becoming staples in criminal trials nationwide" (Jerry Markon, "Poignant Videos of Victims Valid in Court" in The Washington Post, November 29, 2008). Attorneys, according to the article, have objected strongly, claiming the videos are "highly prejudicial."
>
> Rhetorically speaking, such videos indeed do affect the judgment of decision makers, but so would a lack of such communication: Rhetoric involves facts and perspectives not made salient or not put on an agenda.
>
> The Supreme Court has thus far declined to hear legal challenges to the use of said persuasion.
>
> The objection to such videos elicited this objection from a defense attorney: "The determination whether a defendant receives a death sentence turns on the skill of a videographer."
>
> Yes, of course; and without such videos, the sentence will turn on the ability or inability of the prosecutor and defense attorney to tell a moving—read persuasive—story with the defense supported by the criminal. It all depends on where the law wants to focus the question of rhetorical descriptions of the perpetrator, the crimes and their victims. With the "victim impact videos," a new persuader is added to the equation, supporting the victim's interests.

Periodically there are attempts to assess the relative quality of U.S. presidents. Such arguments are a fairly pure form of the agenda/spin model. One chooses facts, makes interpretations, and then sometimes translates such analysis into empirical models, yielding apparently easy comparisons among presidents.

The National Communication Association once provided the 100 best speeches, with a not-unreasonable list (full disclosure: one participant was the author of this book).

(Michael E. Eidenmull, <u>American Rhetoric</u>, website "The Top 100 Speeches").

Historian Thomas Fleming wrote a piece, "Was George W. Bush the Worst President?" in which he says that several polls of historians so stipulate, but that "This baffles me. I've been writing about presidents for a long time. What I know, and what I presume these gentlemen know, doesn't connect."

Of course, all historical judgments are rhetorical judgments: they take selected facts and selected interpretations, and they ignore other facts and other interpretations and come to their persuasive conclusions. Mr. Fleming is a noted historian, so his selected agenda and spin might have persuasive weight.

He argues that John Adams's offer to resign pursuant to incipient hostilities with France in 1798 argues for his being a worse president than George W. Bush. Why wouldn't Adams' military preparedness (F.D.R. may not do so well regarding this criterion and, according to Fleming, others as well, including court-packing and a double-dip depression), successful resolution of the French matter—negotiating a treaty of commerce with Britain—and his personal rectitude count for something? It all depends on what you pay attention to and what you ignore.

I shall dispute Fleming's rhetoric using the agenda/spin model, perhaps because I agree with him. I have already pointed out that this topic arguably is not worth discussing because it is what philosophers would call a "pseudo-issue," whose resolution has no material value to anyone. Further, depending on one's choice of criteria, choice of events during a president's presidency, and the spin one gives to those events, most and perhaps nearly all presidents could be seen as superintending a superior or inferior presidency.

As one of his chosen pieces of evidence, Fleming argues that President Bush was superior to John Adams because Adams offered to resign "so that George [Washington] could resume the job." Fleming asks rhetorically, "How's that for presidential leadership?" We ask, how's that for presidential humility, a counterforce to presidential hubris which arguably got the United States mired in the Vietnam War?

Fleming questions Thomas Jefferson's second term. Why not look instead at President Jefferson's first, stellar term? It's just Fleming's choice of what to make salient.

While examining presidents and candidates, let us look at one of my two favorite columnists (excepting that which he writes on psychiatry) and his use of rhetoric to support John McCain for president in 2008. Rhetoric, as we have stated and restated, is the choice of what facts to make salient and what facts to diminish and sometimes ignore altogether.

Columnist Charles Krauthammer recommended John McCain for president and made a pretty compelling case, especially in retrospect (Charles Krauthammer, "McCain for President," <u>The Washington Post</u>, October 24, 2008).

Rhetorically, one could look at his making salient certain facts of relative preparedness for foreign policy crisis in contrast with Democratic candidate Barack Obama and his (McCain's) honorability and other sundry notions, complete with positive and negative interpretations.

The most compelling argument against voting for McCain, his selection of Sarah Palin for vice presidential nominee, is not even mentioned, although Obama's selection of Biden is. Part of rhetoric, again, is what the persuader chooses to mention or highlight—make salient—and what he or she chooses not to.

On the other side, <u>The New York Times</u> sported an editorial supporting Senator Obama, filled with choices of facts and interpretations friendly to Senator Obama and unfriendly to Senator McCain, in its October 24, 2008, issue, but did not mention—did not *mention*—the surge, during the Iraq war, of George W. Bush, a military thrust that may have radically changed the outcome of the Iraq war itself.

Candidate Obama never mentioned the surge during his campaign; and without a high prestige, non-candidate persuader to bring it up, it never became a salient issue.

Interestingly, this omission proved to be a consistent omission on behalf of those supporting President Obama. On the "FREE for ALL" page of The Washington Post on August 21, 2010, there is an exceptionally insightful letter from the "vice president of external affairs in the Overseas Private Investment Corp. throughout the Bush administration," Christopher Coughlin, who asks incredulously regarding Post coverage of the American troop withdrawal from Iraq. "Is it really possible for you to write a story on the withdrawal of combat troops from Iraq without acknowledging the role of the ["W"] Bush surge in making that exit possible?"

This was an important rhetorical point, indicating the significance of the choices of what facts to include and what facts to ignore in presidential persuasion. President Obama much less frequently omitted *blame* for the Iraqi war on President Bush.

Speaking of the 2008 United States presidential election, in the presidential debates and before, candidate John McCain decided not to make an issue of Barack Obama's relationship with Reverend Jeremiah Wright. What were the motives for the lack of trying to make this potentially election-changing relationship salient? In 2012 Republican Mitt Romney publicly rejected suggestions to resurrect the Wright issue. Again, motives are rarely relevant in persuasive analysis, correctly done, but one's curiosity is certainly aroused as to why Sen. McCain did not attempt to make part of his election agenda the relationship between Barack Obama and Reverend Wright.

Presidential primary and general election debates are thoroughly rhetorical events. As candidates' supporters have become more sophisticated over the years, they rush to media sources immediately following debates in order to win a "debate-debate" of defining how well their candidate did. If a candidate missed too many facts or was seemingly inarticulate, a supporter will focus on the candidate's opponent's alleged weaknesses, or if forced to confront his own candidate's alleged inadequacies, will say something to the effect that "if [X] was not clear on that point, it may be because [opponent's] policies are so faulty that it is hard to articulate all of their weaknesses in just a few minutes."

In 2008, much was made of gaffes by Senator McCain and Governor Sarah Palin, but when allegations were made regarding Senator Joe Biden's gaffes, they were largely ignored by the press, or the interpretation was given that Joe Biden always made little errors, but never missed a step on the big issues. Omission of fact and friendly interpretation of error = rhetorical depiction, as is true of all depictions.


## Conclusion

This chapter outlines the general precepts of the rhetorical view of persuasion in contrast with the situational view. Such a focus should emphasize the crucial role of rhetoric in determining what persuaders and their chosen audiences discuss, what is on their agenda, and interpreting what the agenda, saliences, choices of evidence, etc. mean and what is their significance. The exception to this model occurs only when an auditor or audience is in an all-compelling physical situation which not only demands their attention but makes it inescapable.


## Some Additional Resources

Vatz, R.E. (2009, January). The mythical status of situational rhetoric: implications for rhetorical critics' relevance in the public arena. *The Review of Communication* 9(1), 1-5.

Vatz, R.E. & Weinberg, L.S. (1994). The rhetorical paradigm in psychiatric history: Thomas Szasz and the myth of mental illness. In R. Porter & M. Micale, *Discovering the history of psychiatry*. New York: Oxford University Press.

Vatz, R.E. (2006, Fall). Rhetoric and psychiatry: A Szaszian perspective on a political case study. *Current Psychology* 25(3) pp. 173-181.

Vatz, R.E. (1981, February). More on the rhetorical situation. In Forum Section, *Quarterly Journal of Speech*.

Vatz, R.E. (1973, Summer). The myth of the rhetorical situation. *Philosophy and Rhetoric*.

## Political Persuasion

Virtually all political discourse is persuasively intended. For example, what shall we talk about in a campaign and what does it mean? What (and whose) agenda and what (and whose) spin prevails?

In almost all political contests there are accusations that one or more candidates are "flip-flopping," or taking positions that are inconsistent with past positions. This text takes the position that the success of such claims is almost entirely a function of persuasion.

Take a look at an issue made salient in the 2012 presidential race: whether Massachusetts former Governor Mitt Romney is a flip-flopper. Read the article below for a persuasive analysis of these charges.

> *The Baltimore Sun*
> **Romney flip-flops, and so does Obama**
> *what's wrong with that? The question we should be asking is why politicians change their minds*
>
> *May 04, 2012 by Richard E. Vatz*

What's that you say? You don't hear much about President Barack Obama's flip-flopping?

How about: 1) the Obama reversal regarding child farm-labor regulations; 2) the president's (to quote The New York Times) "revers[ing] his two-year-old order halting new military charges against detainees at Guantánamo Bay, Cuba, permitting military trials to resume with revamped procedures but implicitly admitting the failure of his pledge to close the prison camp" (March 7, 2011); 3) the president's support of former Egyptian president Hosni Mubarak, followed by his throwing him under the bus?

There are plenty more examples, but the inescapable truth is that there is much more mainstream news media coverage of former governor Mitt Romney's "flip-flopping" on health-care, abortion, taking "no-tax" pledges, etc.

This is not intended to assert that Mr. Romney doesn't change positions; it is to point out that almost all politicians do so—and they should. In addition, I would argue that oftentimes the honing of positions does not constitute a major reversal or a flip-flop. Also, I would like to point out that it is impossible for anyone to be perfectly consistent, and, if I may, I should like to quote Walt Whitman's "Do I contradict myself? Very well, then I contradict myself…" (I think he later reconsidered.)

If a politician changes his position—but not the philosophy behind it—it may simply be an evolution of thought. People can and should grow. I certainly hope that one of my least favorite politicians, the late West Virginia Democratic Sen. Robert Byrd, changes his positions from what they were when he created a wing of the Ku Klux Klan in the 1940s.

The salient question is: Does an office holder or an aspiring office holder change his or her positions due to political expediency, and if so, how often?

Mr. Romney changes his position on abortion, but it seems that genuine reflection and study led him to different conclusions. "Romneycare" does have many similarities with Obamacare, but his health policy for Massachusetts—as he has frequently said—is not a national mandate.

He changed his position on whether to sign a "no-tax" pledge. Why? I can find no explanation except political expediency.

President Obama's change of position on President Mubarak seemed to be guided reasonably enough by the exigencies of Egypt's revolution of a sort. What about his position opposing Labor Department regulations on children working with farm equipment? There is about the same number of fatalities now as before, so what led the president to change his mind and allow youngsters to use the heavy equipment? Political expediency, clear and simple.

And how about his Guantánamo turn-around? Well, the proposed change in policy posed a threat to the United States, so his reversal is acceptable, but it would have been nice to hear a confession to the effect that Republicans were correct.

The taunting charge of "flip-flopping," directed predominantly against Mitt Romney, appears to reflect political bias in reporting. It is an exaggerated issue, but not irrelevant.

Regardless, the differential between the two key presidential candidates on this issue is not reasonably dispositive in determining anyone's vote.

I wrote the following blogs in Maryland's "Red Maryland" to characterize rhetorically the 2012 presidential election. The election was a struggle for agenda and spin, and the initial focus, of course, was on the struggle for agenda between Barack Obama and Mitt Romney.

### *Mitt Romney's Gaffe-seekers and Their Success*

*—Richard E. Vatz*

The paradox of writing critically about the consistent "Gotcha" strategy of President Barack Obama's presidential campaign is that to write about it is to accede to the effort to create distractions from his destructive economic polities (and to a lesser extent his disastrous superintending of the "lead from behind" foreign policy that has eviscerated American influence).

The far-left *Mother Jones* magazine released a video of Gov. Romney at a fundraiser for large donors in which he said, as quoted by *The Baltimore Sun*, "There are 47 percent of the people who will vote for the president, no matter what. All right, there are 47 percent who are with him who are dependent upon government, who believe that they are victims…they will vote for this president no matter what…these are people who pay no income tax…[M]y job is not to worry about these people…I'll never convince them they should take personal responsibility and care for their lives."

Some points of refutation of the Democrat's spin that these quotes mean that Gov. Romney has "disdainfully" voiced his contempt for half the population:

1.  Any candidate among donors tends to inflate his rhetoric; but it is a legitimate point that America, through decreasing entitlements, has become a more dependent nation, and this influences voting habits to reduce the individual initiative. It does not literally mean that Gov. Romney believes that 47% of the nation is looking for handouts.

2.  This is yet another attempt of Democratic sympathizers to control the campaign agenda to substitute Gov. Romney's tin ear, unpublished taxes, carrying his dog atop a van, and allegedly premature criticism of the president's Middle East and North Africa policies for discussions of the aforementioned economy and lack of any semblance of an effective foreign policy.

3.  That 47% of the public pays no federal income tax would be a telling surprise to the public; if polled, according to my Towson students, the general public would have guessed the figure to be around 10%. There is little beyond the horserace and Romney gaffes and general rhetorical clumsiness which is covered by NBC, ABC, and MSNBC.

I naïvely told some students that no national rhetorician could control the national agenda for four or more months leading up to a presidential election.

In retrospect, I may have been incorrect.

*Sunday, September 30, 2012*
**The "Presidential Agenda Election" of 2012**

*—Richard E. Vatz*

"In circumstances like that, there are efforts made, sometimes desperate efforts, to change the subject."— White House Press Secretary Jay Carney, claiming that Gov. Mitt Romney's videotaped statement to the effect that 47% of the country is increasingly dependent on government is what the country should discuss, not the issue of President Obama's support of redistribution of wealth. The 2012 presidential election, more than any previous election in history, will turn on what issue(s) acquire agenda status for the voting electorate of America, and perhaps only the voting electorate of swing states.

Who determines what the issues are in a presidential campaign? Why is a topic such as the president's non-secret videotapes support of redistribution of wealth changing the subject from a legitimate one to an illegitimate one?

For over 35 years I have argued in my field of Mass Communication and Communication Studies that persuasion (or rhetoric) is about 2 things: "agenda creation," the competition to determine what persuaders and audiences discuss; and "spin," trying to infuse interpretation, meaning and significance for audiences into the agenda made salient for them.

This year's election is the perfect application of this theory of persuasion. In my book, *The Only Authentic Book of Persuasion*, there is a 2012 cartoon by Ed Gamble of the King Features Syndicate in which a chap representing "Gay Groups" is sitting next to the president, who is supporting "same sex marriage," and the president says, "Let's hope this evolves to be another issue that distracts voters from the economy."

The unemployment rate appears to be permanently mired in 8-plus percentage territory, or at least until the end of the current administration. The economy is disastrous. Foreign policy choices arguably threaten instability across the Middle East and North Africa and possibly allow an Iranian game-changer in the calculus of nuclear-armed countries and its geo-political consequences.

So what issues have the Democrats tried to substitute for the economy on the national agenda? Mitt Romney's unreleased tax returns, Todd Akin's ignorant superstition that a "legitimate" rape cannot result in pregnancy, the fiction that Gov. Romney's policies at Bain Capital led to a woman's death, the alleged Republican "War on Women," Gov. Romney's claim that he has an uphill climb to receive the votes of beneficiaries of government largess, and other even less significant matters.

In a recent *USA Today* interview, Gov. Romney said, intriguingly enough, "There are plenty of weaknesses that I have, and I acknowledge that, but the attacks that have come have been so misguided…[and] have been so dishonest that they surprised me. I thought they might go after me on things that were accurate that I've done wrong, instead of absurd things."

It is the essence of political persuasion: make the topic you want salient, salient…and try to de-emphasize topics that redound to your detriment.

This has been done before in presidential elections, but never so preposterously or clownishly, and it has never been so effective, except maybe in 2004; but even then, the Bush Administration met opposing arguments on seminal issues head-on while focusing somewhat on Sen. John Kerry's wavy record and alleged flip-flopping.

Many in the media have a critical role in helping to determine with what issues they confront candidates, and the Democratic agenda seems in large part to be fine with them, perhaps because personal attacks are less complicated than economic and foreign policy analysis.

This election concerned, as all do, the interpretation of issues, but first and foremost it was an election concerning what is the presidential election agenda.

The short shrift given to the inarguably important agenda of economic and foreign policy issues constitutes a rhetorical victory for those favoring a non-substantive American presidential election.

Presidential debates have historically had significant effects on the outcome of the presidential elections only when the elections were close ones. This is due to the fact that by the time such debates occur, in October of an election year, public opinion, as measured by the public opinion polls, is already mostly solidified. This is in stark contrast to primary debates, which can affect public opinion polls quite significantly due in part to the public's not being heavily engaged in primary elections but more substantially to the lack of intensity and lack of knowledge regarding non-incumbent candidates in national elections.

What follows is a short analysis of presidential debate persuasion from 1960, when they began, to the 2012 presidential debates, again, from Maryland's Red Maryland blog.

*Monday, November 5, 2012*
**Presidential Debates: Their Entire History in About 700 Words, and the Impact of Obama-Romney Debates in 2012.**

*—Richard E. Vatz*

The presidential election is tomorrow, and we have had three presidential debates and one vice-presidential debate. The vice-presidential debate arguably served to establish that Rep. Paul Ryan and Vice President Joe Biden would not be an issue in the presidential sweepstakes.

Let us speculate on the role of debates in presidential campaigns with first some perspective on a prevailing myth: presidential debates have little effect on presidential races and never have. Truth: There is no way to be certain regarding the effect of said debates on the presidential voting outcome, but arguably in the 11 years of presidential debates 1960, 1976-2012), they may have had a significant effect all years but 1984, 1988, and 1996.

In Reagan' second campaign in 1984, he has a miserable debate. Confused and unfocused, he lost one point in the polls after his bad first debate showing.

In 1988 Michael Dukakis, contrary to popular belief regarding a major debate gaffe regarding his diffidence when CNN's Bernard Shaw asked him his view on capital punishment if his (Dukakis's) wife were killed, was losing significantly by the time of the debates.

In 1996 Bob Dole, intent on demonstrating he was no longer the nasty man of the 1976 Vice Presidential debates, offended no one and was a perfect couplet to his excellent-but-passive vice presidential running mate, Jack Kemp.

When were debates arguably quite different?

Before presidential debates in 1960, President Kennedy was little known; but his visuals and rhetorical brilliance in the 1960 debates overwhelmed the irritating, television-averse Richard Nixon.

In 1976 President Gerald Ford and his pardoning of Nixon, along with a memorable debate gaffe on Eastern Europe, led to his undoing; in 1980 debates made Americans comfortable with the previously perceived-as-radical Governor Ronald Reagan. Jimmy Carter's economy and Iran-linked hostage weakness coupled with Gov. Reagan's debate-tested "There you go again" and "Are you better off today than you were for years ago?" won him the election going away.

In 1992 Ross Perot and Gov. Bill Clinton ganged up on George H. W. Bush—and *that*, not the president's looking at his watch, lost him the debates and the presidency.

In 2000 the multi-personality debate persona of Vice President Gore, not the Florida vote count, lost him the presidency to George W. Bush, although the latter was a weak debater.

In 2004 the expectation was that debates would destroy George W. Bush, but John Kerry—he of the flip-flop reputation (and currently likely chief purveyor of the Romney flip-flop accusation by President Obama in debates)—was never convincing that he was no longer the irresponsible, pre-eminent anti-war protester.

In 2008 Sen. John McCain was so intent on being perceived as a good and fair man (see Dole, Robert, 1996) that he didn't bring up Sen. Barack Obama's questionable associate until the third debate. Why didn't he emphasize President Obama's utter inexperience more? Probably he thought it would offend someone—oh, and Sarah Palin's failing paroxysm of popularity was foreseen by all who despaired over this unvetted in-your-face choice who faltered in the Vice President debate to a reasonably unsmiling Joe Biden. By the way, whatever happened to him?

So, here is what the 2012 debates did for the 2012 candidates: First, the well-traveled, but seriously unknown, Mitt Romney became more than an abstract symbol of supercilious nobility. President Obama showed he could come back from inexplicable debate lethargy to fight for his presidency. And, finally, the debates revealed that it was an election about two things: Gov. Romney's claim that President Obama has failed economically versus President Obama's claim that Gov. Romney is a chameleon who cannot be trusted in the Oval Office (see Kerry, John, 2004).

The 2012 presidential election was won by the Barack Obama-Joe Biden team over the Mitt Romney-Paul Ryan team for multifarious reasons. To understand the key reason, however, *effective persuasion*, one needs to look at Barack Obama and his media supporters along with the poor rhetorical showing of Mitt Romney in establishing the presidential election agenda and the spin of the constituents of that agenda.

Without oversimplifying, the primary dispositive rhetorical election-vote-changer, in this writer's opinion, was in their foreign policy debate the inability of Governor Romney to follow up on his first election debate win by forcing President Obama to defend his failures in that area. Moreover, in the "spin" area, Obama ridiculed Romney over his concern about Russia as a "geo-political" threat.

President Obama attempted to paint Romney as somehow out-of-touch with 21st century geo-politics, suggesting (ironically, as we now know) that al-Qaeda was a bigger threat than Russia. "You said Russia. Not al-Qaeda. You said Russia," Obama said regarding biggest threats. Then came this persuasively telling blast:

"The 1980s are now calling to ask for their foreign policy back because…the Cold War's been over for 20 years."

Setting aside the fact that while Obama suggested that al-Qaeda was the number-one geo-political threat in the world and later claimed that the terrorist group had been "decimated" and was "on the run" only to learn that it is now (2014) stronger and controls more territory that at any time in its history, could this snide comment to Romney look any more foolish than it now does?

This was the second time in 2014 that former Republican candidates—ridiculed at the time for their foreign policy observations—have been proved right about Russia: Sarah Palin, no candidate favorite of the author, predicted in 2008 that under a weak Obama, Russia would be tempted to invade Ukraine.

In fact, all political persuasion is a function of who has the ability to determine the salience-agenda of issues and the meaning-spin of issues for relevant audiences.

*baltimoresun.com*
**A better debate [Commentary]**
*To make debates more useful (and tolerable) for the watchers, a few rules are in order*

*By Richard E. Vatz and Lee S. Weinberg*
*6:00AM EDT, June 15, 2014*

Watching political debates—local, regional and national—the keen observer will note that the venues are like baseball stadiums: tailored for the advantage of a few, with parameters sometimes varying widely to satisfy certain politicians, citizens, media outlets, etc.

It is not an exaggeration to say that no format has ever satisfied all observers, and some of them satisfy very few. Some of the complaints there are too many or too few debates for a primary or general election; they are too long or too short; there is too much or too little restriction on time for answers; there is over-or under-involvement of moderators; too many candidates are included (or excluded)-and so on.

Some even complain, although this is less articulated as debates have become an accepted part of the political landscape, that debating is not a valid method by which to evaluate candidates; being quick on your feet in answering limited questions does not predict prudent governing.

True enough: political debates are not an unalloyed good, despite the fact that in recent years even odds-on favorites have felt the pressure or just a democratic need to debate. Maryland U.S. Rep Dutch Ruppersberger always debates if his opponent wishes to, but there is nothing race-wise to be gained by him doing so. Decades ago, though, front runners would not have given their opponents the stage, especially if doing so would make a relative unknown appear to be a sufficiently significant figure who would then have a chance for victory.

In 1960, Richard Nixon made the political mistake of his life when the vice president debated on national television with 43-year old John F. Kennedy, a relatively unknown Massachusetts senator.

Still, with the new presumption in favor of political debating in all major (and many minor) races and also assuming the value of debates for electorate to make wise voting decisions, herein please find some suggestions for future debates, for both primary and general elections.

- Debates should be limited to candidates with 15 percent of more support in the public opinion polls. Yes, this can be arbitrary and a problem when someone a few points below the mark appears to be making a move, but to allow anyone and everyone who wants to participate dilutes discussion significantly and disallows serious policy discussion. Ross Perot, who won 19 percent of the vote, was a major candidate in 1992 and perhaps changed that election's results. Don't like that? We didn't. Too bad—it was good for democracy.

- Moderators should be punctiliously neutral, to the point of not questioning factual representations of debate participants whatsoever; that is the job of the other debaters. In the 2012 CNN presidential debate, Candy Crowley singularly disputed Gov. Mitt Romney's claim that President Barack Obama did not initially say the attack in Benghazi constituted "terrorism." In doing so, she unfairly flummoxed the surprised challenger and strengthened for herself and CNN a reputation for political bias.

- Debate organizers should arrange at least two, but no more than three, debates of an hour each on electronic media. No candidate may speak for more than 90 seconds per question, including allowing for one follow-up by each. We have never seen a debate that required more than an hour. as a debate goes on, diminishing returns always creep in.

- Have audience members—who must not be allowed to cheer or else they will be removed—submit questions in writing. There is no informational advantage to giving a publicity-hungry member of the audience a chance to argue with a candidate. In addition, a fair moderator can edit a question to the advantage of a good substantive inquiry.

- Finally, a substantive bit of advice to accompany to advisories above: When candidates make spending or taxing recommendations, they should include—or their opponents should demand—answers to the following questions:

    a. What will those cost, and who will pay for it?

    b. What is the likelihood that you will get necessary support for this initiative?

    c. What evidence exists that the expenditure will have the result(s) you predict?

    d. By when do you expect to see the results?

    e. Will you retract public spending if the results are not produced?

We often wonder if the public realizes that there is minimal disagreement on outcomes in policies—only, or mostly, on how to reach those outcomes.

Those recommendations would make for better issue exchanges and would also create more equitable and democratic political persuasion.

# Chapter II

# THE MYTHICAL STATUS OF SITUATIONAL RHETORIC: IMPLICATIONS FOR RHETORICAL CRITICS' RELEVANCE IN THE PUBLIC ARENA

THIRTY-FIVE YEARS AGO I argued that portraying rhetoric as the inexorable results of real situational demands (as opposed to competitive persuasion), creating perceptions of situational demands, would regulate the field to secondary disciplinary status and ethical irrelevance. Since then, this prediction has been largely fulfilled, but a change in perspective can make rhetoric a primary study with ethical significance.

*Keywords: Rhetoric; Persuasion; Political Commentary; Responsibility; Salience; Meaning; Agenda; Spin; Framing*

Thirty-five years after I wrote (The Myth of the Rhetorical Situation" (1973) and 40 years after Lloyd Bitzer wrote "The Rhetorical Situation" (1968), I thought this might be a propitious moment to reflect on some important academic implications of those two articles.

This article of reflection is not meant to be yet another refinement of the arguments therein, but instead an overview of what the implications of this seminal clash in perspectives have meant to the field of rhetoric's view of the relationship between situations and rhetoric and the study of persuasion. This is also the title of a course, "Persuasion," that I have successfully taught and which has been the focus of many teaching awards for about 35 years. I should add, parenthetically, that this dispute has significantly informed the three areas of personal expertise on which I have written, consulted, and commented in media for decades: political rhetoric, psychiatric rhetoric, and media criticism.

My purpose is to explore an omnipresent concept in life—the choice of what we talk about and the choices of what it means—that has critical importance to rhetorical practice. In Plato's day, whether one sided with Plato or the Sophists was not an idle matter, of importance only to the intellectuals of the day. It was, instead, a matter of "life and death" with respect to how one might interpret reality and enact values in the world.

Lloyd Bitzer's "The Rhetorical Situation" (1968) argued that rhetoric was situationally based, which made rhetoric a pre-determined result of whatever the reality of the situation was: "Rhetorical discourse is called into existence by situation" (p. 9); "So controlling is situation that we should consider it the very ground of rhetorical activity" (p. 5); and, most unambiguously, "[T]he situation controls the rhetorical response" (p. 4).

My "Myth" piece, as a counterpoint to Bitzer's view, was based on the following three premises: The study of rhetoric has always been integral to, and perhaps synonymous with, the study of persuasion. Rhetorical study and persuasion encompass necessarily the depiction of reality to chosen audiences through chosen media. In all of its forms such representation involves a rhetor's choice or choices in trying to determine what should have the attention of chosen audiences, and what the chosen situations should mean to those audiences. In short, discrete "situations" are largely mythical concepts, rhetorically based and circumscribed (Vatz, 1973, 1981, 2005, 2006).

I argued in "The Myth of the Rhetorical Situation" that, contrary to Bitzer's arguments, situations do not produce rhetoric, but rather that rhetors strategically promote salience and meanings for chosen audiences, and when successful, these pass for real situations to which it seems we must pay attention.

As I argued in the "Myth" (1973) piece:

The essential question to be addressed is: What is the relationship between rhetoric and situations? It will not be surprising that I take the converse position of each of Bitzer's major statements regarding this relationship. For example: I would not say 'rhetoric is situational,' but situations are rhetorical; not '…exigence strongly invites utterance,' but utterance strongly invites exigence; not '…rhetorical discourse… does obtain its character-as-rhetorical from the situation which generates it,' but situations obtain their character from the rhetoric which surrounds them or creates them (pp.158-159).

Finally:

Rhetors choose or do not choose to make salient situations, facts, events, etc. This may be the *sine qua non* of rhetoric: the art of linguistically or symbolically creating salience. After salience is created, the situation must be translated into meaning (p. 160).

Honesty dictates the observation that if the competition between these perspectives has been a 35-year footrace, it has been won by Bitzer's philosophy. More articles and professionals in our field cite his situational perspective (although quite a few use the "Myth" perspective, and some do without realizing it) than my rhetorical perspective. The situational outlook implies that rhetoricians qua rhetoricians have a perspicacious view of reality that allows them to dictate to audiences what the hierarchy of situational importance is in our society, indeed the world; and then they can declaim on such matters and analyze the rhetoric which they claim inexorably follows from what they arbitrarily define as controlling situations and/or exigencies.

## The Question of Relevance

The situational take on rhetoric has a presumptive starting point, and it has crucial and material political and academic implications for our field. Professors of rhetoric and communication who reflect that view in their teaching, publishing, and commenting can assume that their rhetorical analyses merely reflect the truth as dictated by the situation, a 'truth' which in actuality only corresponds to the values and perceptions of the professor.

There is overwhelming competition to being able to interpret reality, particularly in the political realm, and there are those who have a much better claim with more significant audiences to be able to perform such interpretation than we rhetoricians. The reason that rhetoricians have never preponderantly been the primary sources that media consult is that we are just one of many competitors interpreting reality. Often we are looked at as purveyors of "mere rhetoric," which perception the situational point of view stated above fosters. Thus, assuming as valid the situational root of rhetoric also means that rhetoricians, although they are often aligned with the political zeitgeist of academia, must compete with other high-ethos sources in political or social commentary which, again, have more *bona fide* credentials to be able to sort out reality: political scientists, historians, journalists, bloggers, etc. In fact, the fragmentation of prominent sources of rhetoric demands even more the approach to rhetoric argued in the "Myth" piece. Imagine how increasingly irrelevant situationally-grounded rhetoricians' depictions and interpretations of reality must seem to political principals, political professionals, and even average citizens.

We rhetoricians and political communication experts thus end up being second-class citizens by playing the more accepted experts' sport on their home territory, and much of what we do constitutes an embarrassing redundancy. A minority in our field is much sought after and excels in the public arena, but the rank-and-file cannot burst through because they have no unique perspective or philosophy to offer, or else they have a viewpoint which is understandably not seen as sufficiently different from that of other standard academics.

Moreover, most of the rhetoricians who are successful in often being cited and quoted by media are those who claim, whether they realize it or not, that we have some special perspicacity in ascertaining not what issues impinge on our reality, but how rhetors compete to make salient their chosen agendas and how they compete for interpretation or spin.

Thus, the temporary victory of the realists of our field is a Pyrrhic victory.

Fortunately, though, the victory cannot be accurately claimed as completed, because not only is the competition a marathon and not a sprint, it is a never-ending marathon.

Over the last few decades, several terms have emerged in the public lexicon which correspond to the terms "creating salience" and "creating meaning." These terms are, respectively, "agenda" creation (creating salience) and "framing" and "spin" (creating meaning). The term "agenda" has been popularized and has come to signify the issues that a given sources wishes to be discussed. The terms "framing" and "spin" creating have come to mean a strategic slant put on information directed to various audiences, with the former term seen as less tendentious than the latter. The terms "spin doctors," derived from "spin," has come to be a pejorative phrase referring to allegedly base rhetors who consciously inject false infusions of meaning. All of these concepts could have been part of an acknowledged lexicon of rhetorical analysis if the majority of our field had not opted for the anti-rhetorical philosophy dictated by "The Rhetorical Situation." It is, incidentally, difficult to account for the motives which have led to our sociologically devastating majority choosing the situational perspective: it is partly the field's hierarchical support for that perspective, but it may also be that a situational perspective allows the academic to claim his or her interpretation of reality is superior. Unfortunately, again, the situational choice leaves rhetoricians competitively without a distinctive raison d'être.

Courses and books about persuasion so critical to rhetorical study do not even debate the foregoing. Many books about persuasion do not even reference either perspective, despite the integral connections of the battle of this wholly rhetorical study.

One of the interesting questions that arises as regards to the rhetoric-situation debate is whether there is a liberal-conservative divide attending this ostensibly politics-free difference in viewpoint. Bitzer's examples in his 1968 article tended to be conventionally liberal: he saw as a rhetorical hero John F. Kennedy, not

Dwight David Eisenhower; he saw a rhetorical exigence or problem in his original article "the pollution of our air," but not the apposite profit-reducing constraints on a then major steel industry produced by enforced reduction of pollution. Scholars in rhetoric in fact typically use the rhetorical situation to foster liberal points of view. Peruse major rhetoric and communication journals and notice many conservative United States presidents or politicians or actors in general are written about negatively, in contrast to their liberal counterparts.

In the "Myth" piece and subsequent writings, I have argued that one of the paramount issues in rhetoric is the responsibility that the source of rhetoric has for the agenda he/she has chosen, and the interpretation of that agenda. President George W. Bush's insistence of Iraq's salience and being part of his agenda can reasonably be part of that which is cited as his legacy. However, how did he rhetorically make the case in Iraq's inextricability from the issue of terrorism, and how did he successfully depict for national and international audiences, the "War on Terror" as actually a "war?"

Is "war on terror" a persuasive appeal without a definable enemy?

These issues are appropriate fodder for rhetorical analysis, according to the "Myth" perspective, but do not lend themselves to our field's performing situational analysis. In fact, there is nothing inherently liberal or conservative in either approach that lends itself to liberal or conservative argument. The essentials of each type of argument are apolitical, but those of the situational approach are more easily used to promote a political point of view—usually liberal when the scholar is in academia—whereas the rhetorical approach encourages more disinterested analysis and criticism.

Examples regarding the differences between situational and rhetorical analysis are literally inexhaustible, but there has been recently an especially revealing debate which may serve as synecdoche for some of the preceding observations. The matter concerns capital punishment and the claim that execution of criminals creates a new victim class: the relatives of the deceased perpetrator (Associated Press 2006). This new focus (creation of salience-agenda) on a matter heretofore relatively unimportant to many of us, states that even though members of the families of convicted felons haven't done anything wrong (selected facts and interpretation), those family members are "victims too" (interpretation/spin). This is not a new phenomenon, although a relatively new group, Murder Victims' Families for Human Rights, an anti-death penalty group, has written a text called "Creating More Victims: How Executions Hurt the Families Left Behind." Thus, through a new creation of salience and agenda accompanied by a new infusion of meaning and spin (and framing of the concept of "victim"), a new persuasive action is attempted: to stop capital punishment.

Can the public be persuaded that some of the real victims in murders are the relatives of the murderers themselves?

The "Myth's" "salience-meaning" or now perhaps "agenda-framing-spin" perspective on rhetoric is one which makes rhetorical study a primary study. The situational perspective argues that there is a reality which dictates that to which we pay attention and what its significance is. The latter perspective puts rhetoricians in the weak position of claiming in the face of higher ethos experts what the political reality is, and what depiction serves as the entire basis for what rhetorical analysis has to offer; my colleague, a historian of rhetoric Dr. Marlana Portolano, says typically this approach is a grossly 'incomplete theory,' which 'left unexamined, can calcify in any academic discipline.' In contrast, the former rhetorical perspective focuses on the study of persuasion and makes our discipline a more important player in the national scene of politics, a player that offers a unique critical perspective for analyzing and commenting on a persuaders' choices of that to which to give rhetorical focus and meaning, framing, and/or spin they argue for their chosen saliences or agenda.

According to what one can reasonably infer from the "situational" theory of rhetoric, who or what is responsible for the national agenda of issues in America? Cite some examples.

Is the field of persuasion and rhetoric more important or less important if the salience-agenda/meaning-spin model is subordinated to the situational model? Provide some examples.

## References

Associated Press. (2006, December 25). Often criminals' families are victims, too. *The Baltimore Sun*, p. 6A.

Bitzer, L. (1968). The rhetorical situation. *Philosophy and Rhetoric*, 1, 1-14.

Vatz, R. E. (1973). The myth of the rhetorical situation. *Philosophy and Rhetoric*, 6, 154-161. Vatz, R. E. (1981). Vatz on Patton and Bitzer. *Quarterly Journal of Speech*, 67, 95-99.

Vatz, R. E. (2005). The article rewrite assignment. *The Successful Professor*, 4. Retrieved December 21, 2007, from http://pages.towson.edu/vatz/rewrite2006two.pdf.

Vatz, R. E. (2006). Rhetoric and psychiatry: A Szaszian perspective on a political case study. *Current Psychology*, 25, 173ff.

# Chapter III

# THE ARTICLE REWRITE ASSIGNMENT: UNDERSTANDING PERSUASION

❖

ONE PARTICULAR ASSIGNMENT THAT I have given for over forty years has had a strong effect on the popularity of my courses and teaching in general. This assignment, which has been required in every one of my advanced "Persuasion" courses since 1973, is called simply the "Article Rewrite Assignment." It stems from the most provocative and reprinted article I have written in my career, "The Myth of the Rhetorical Situation" (Vatz: 1973), published in the preeminent journal in rhetorical theory, *Philosophy and Rhetoric*. The article was the antithesis of an earlier article in the same journal called "The Rhetorical Situation" (Bitzer: 1968).

My article argues that, contrary to the philosophy articulated in "The Rhetorical Situation," rhetoric creates, rather than reflects, reality through a struggle for salience and meaning, roughly equivalent to today's concepts of establishing an agenda and infusing a spin.

For just one illustration: according to the perspective argued in the "The Rhetorical Situation," the rhetoric surrounding recent U.S. wars in Iraq and Afghanistan was the results of specifiable and real components of those wars; the components inescapably engendered the rhetoric. By the perspective argued in the "Myth of the Rhetorical Situation," however, the rhetoric surrounding the wars was a result of decisions by major players to make salient certain points and infuse them with the desired meaning. In the "Myth" the rhetors have responsibility for what they make salient and the meaning infused in the saliency. Thus, the relevance and significance and even the facticity of not finding weapons of mass destruction were rhetorically manufactured for different audiences.

This assignment requires students to choose an opinionated article in the popular press and *reverse* the essence of its position. While I maintain that this reversal could be applied to articles in the news pages, I direct the students to article or reviews of books, movies, CDs and plays in *Time*, *Newsweek*, *The Washington Post* (Style Page), and *The New York Times*, as well as other newspapers and magazines. I also recommend that the students consider restaurant and dance reviews, for these also may recommend themselves superbly for this assignment. The students may find articles through the internet but must provide paper copies so I may see in a consistent way what is done by the source of the article, including layout, pictures locations, etc.

Reprinted by permission of The Successful Professor.

If the assignment can be summed up in two words, the words would be "persuasive reinterpretation." The somewhat complicated rules of the assignment, to make it consistent with the perspective on rhetoric they have learned, are as follows:

The student may not change facts (or the plot, if it is a movie or play review) of the article. Where there is subjectivity, it may be reversed. Thus, in reversing a negative movie review of Dustin Hoffman's acting, the student may not claim that Dustin Hoffman is tall, but *may* say that "even Mr. Hoffman's acting in *Ishtar* showed under-appreciated aspects of brilliance." If a negative original says, "The singer's range no longer could accommodate the high notes," the writer may not say "His range was equal to that of 20 years ago," but he or she *may* say, "The beauty of his sounds more than compensated for any small loss of range he experienced over the years." In reversing a positive dance review, "fast dancing" may be portrayed as "frenetic," but not "slow." The reversals must follow the original practically line by line with reversals occurring in sequence. The changes must have a material point to them: if a book review starts out by saying that the reviewer woke up on a sunny morning, the student may not say that the brightness of the day made it difficult to drive. But if the review is positive, the writer may say, in reversing the piece, that the "sunniness of the day was in stark contrast to the interview which followed."

Changes must be plausible, reasonable, and *substantial*; no credit is given to the adding of the word *not* to make an affirmative sentence negative. Students may add pictures from other sources and/or reverse the captions on pictures in the original.

The reversing of the original must be consistent; if a negative original concedes a positive point, in the reversal that point must be made *more* positive. Thus, if the original says, "Despite their short-sightedness, the Republicans have managed to win most of the presidential elections since 1968," the student may write that "Due to their understanding of the electorate, the Republicans have won all but two of the presidential elections since 1968 in which the Democratic nominee has been a liberal."

Quotations may be eliminated or truncated, and one or two may be substituted, but in no case may the intended meaning be subverted or the words changed. Thus, if an original positive review of *Spiderman II* quotes movie reviewer Roger Ebert as saying "Tobey McGuire in a uniquely capable actor, but is at times in over his head," the student may not write that Ebert says that McGuire "lacks capability." He *may* say that Ebert sees McGuire as "in over his head." A couple excellent examples of recent note by students in sections of "Persuasion" over the last decade or so:

## Original (Large: 2004)

### Going to XS is, well, fun

…The breakfast food is kind of ordinary (which may be just what you want in breakfast food). For instance, the omelet—overcooked—comes with white bread toast, little cubes of fried potatoes and a small cup of cut-up fruit. No surprises there. But the coffee is good and strong, and you'd never guess the maple chicken sausage patties aren't pork. The sushi, however, is anything but ordinary. There's none of the minimalist Japanese things going on. A maki roll like Chorishi's Fire is an extravagant creation decorated with orchids and feathery sprays or celery leaves. The crispy bits of shrimp tempura folded in with avocado and tuna offer up a startling interplay of textures and flavors, none of them pedestrian. Not to mention the drizzle of spicy pink sauce trailing over the rice…

## Student Rewrite
*by Elizabeth Broccolino:*

Going to XS is, well, depressing...

The breakfast food is the same as what you could make in your own home, sans the tacky atmosphere. The omelet—overcooked, no less—comes with such Dennyesque sides as bread, cubes of potatoes and a cup of fruit. Suddenly, the restaurant's banality rears its ugly head. But luckily the coffee is so heavily dosed with caffeine that you'll be too jittery to notice that the sausage patties aren't even real pork. And then there's the sushi. Destroying the tradition of the Japanese delicacy, American gluttony takes over. A maki roll, inexplicably named "Chiroshi's Fire," is a tawdry contrivance of sushi, haphazardly topped with flowers and leaves of celery, hiding the disappointment of the sushi itself. The crisp—no, the teeth-shattering—little crumbs of shrimp tempura mixed with avocado and tuna horrify the palette with their obvious incompatibility. They cannot even leave the rice alone, squirting a sort of Pepto-Bismol colored sauce over it.

## Original (Gorelick, 2010)

Authentic Flavors of Milan

...The space is still a dream, and you can see why those opera evenings Sotto Sopra produces have become so successful. With its crimson curtains, vibrant murals and ornate furnishings, its theatricality is enveloping. But it's very warm and comfortable here; keen attention to lighting and music has much to do with that.

Over the years, Bosio brought in to run his kitchen a series of chefs, some of them from his native Milan, and usually for only a year at a stretch. A double exception was Bill Crouse, who stayed for three years and folded a little Maryland flavor into the Northern Italian menu. Crouse's departure a few months ago set the stage for the entrance of a new chef. And in a dynamic turn, it was Bosio himself.

## Student Rewrite
*by Noreen Mughal:*

A Taste of Milan Leaves Much to be Desired

The place can be likened to a nightmare, and it's quite inexplicable why those opera evenings Sotto Sopra encourages have achieved even a temporary audience. Deep blood-red curtains, excessive, loud murals and overly dramatic furnishings accentuate the pomposity one might associate with theater. It is so oppressively hot inside that one barely pays heed to the poor lighting, only to the music that unapologetically violates the ear.

A series of chefs were imported from Italy, by Bosio, but many were unwilling to stay. The exception was Bill Crouse, who felt that adding Maryland flavor to the North Italian menu might somehow salvage it. Crouse's decision to quit unraveled yet another unwelcome surprise for Sotto Sopra, the owner now turned chef.

## Original (Ligaya Mishan, 2001)

### Noshing Down Mulberry Street NYTimes

Do not snub Frito pie ($5). This Tex-Mex snack, recreated from childhood memories by Gabe Thompson, the chef of L'Artusi, should be the feast's sleeper hit. It comes in a Fritos bag, which is snipped open so that chili con carne can be ladled inside. You think its a joke, and then your eyes go wide.

\* \* \*

But you wanted Italian. Rubirosa, a local pizzeria, plays it straight with a mini braciole sandwich ($5). In one bite is the essence of a spaghetti dinner, garlic bread included.

## Student Rewrite

*by Grace Manlove:*

### Famine is Better Than This Feast

Please ignore the Frito Pie. This humiliating Tex-Mex fabrication, a recreation from childhood memories of Gabe Thompson which should have stayed in the past, is the feast's biggest fault. This Tex-Mex disaster comes in a reused Fritos bag which has been lopped off at the top for the chili con carne to be slopped into. You think it is a joke, and then you pay five dollars for it.

If Italian is what you came for, stay away from Rubirosa, a local pizzeria, giving insult to the Italian treat of braciole by transforming it into mini sandwiches. In one bite the sandwich tries for a spaghetti dinner, including greasy garlic break acting as a roll.

## Original (Kliman, 2012)

### High on Thai

It was inevitable that Johnny Monis, the young chef who pilots Komi, Washington's best restaurant, would eventually open a second place. The questions were when and what—questions that Monis, as idiosyncratic as he is brilliant, seemed in no hurry to answer…

His second act, Little Serow, turns out to be a 28-seat Thai restaurant in an English basement with no sign at its entrance. Festooned with hanging light bulbs and sporting a DIY-looking paint job the color of crème de menthe, the restaurant looks like the sort of project you see when an ambitious sous chef breaks free and starts his own place.

It feels like it, too. The young staffers, all onetime Komi employees, light up with smiles when you walk in—grateful, it seems, that you've discovered them. It may be the warmest welcome in town…

One of the wonders of Komi, where dinner ends with spit-roasted shared plates, is that it imposes on diners a communal sensibility. Little Serow couldn't be more different in its aims, but it's clear that Monis doesn't merely want to feed us delicious things. In the mediterranean manner—or in this case, the northern Thai manner—he wants us to slow down and linger. Dinner is seven dishes, served family style, for $45 (they change somewhat from week to week, and there are no substitutions), and the pacing is closer to that of a tasting table than of a neighborhood Thai joint…

The $45 price is more than twice what you'd expect to pay at most Thai restaurants—though about a third the cost of dining at Komi. But it affords Monis the buying power to procure the freshest meats and produce…

The vegetables aren't only accents; they're utensils. The same goes for the basket of sticky rice, which is meant to be rolled into balls and used to scoop up salads and sauces and enfold the various meats that make up the latter half of the meal.

It's nearly impossible to zip through dinner eating this way. The cooking demands that you take the time to explore and savor it—the interplay of textures, the subtleties that unfold after the initial wave of heat.

The biggest surprise about Little Serow, beyond the fact that Monis decided a northern Thai restaurant should be his vehicle for branching out, is how straightforward he is…

[Monis'] "charred, hammered" beef would have made a great steak. Instead, he marinates it, slices it thin, and piles it in a heaping mound on the plate…[I]n other hands, the kaffir-lime-laced pork sausage might have provided a starting point for a more elaborate dish, but Monis opts for simplicity, creating a light, almost spongy texture and giving the sausage a casing that pops at the first bite…

Intensely personal undertakings like this are often vanity projects that can be doomed by seriousness and self-congratulation. That Monis avoids self indulgence is a testament to his devotion to the cuisine and to his considerable skills as a cook. His love of discovery is palpable. After seven courses over several hours, mine was, too.

From *The Washingtonian*, February 2012 by Todd Kliman. Copyright © 2012 by *The Washingtonian*. Reprinted by permission.

# Student Rewrite

*by Amanda Frye:*

## Price Too High for Thai

It was a foregone conclusion that Johnny Monis, head chef of Washington's Komi, would eventually try again. The questions were when and what—questions that Monis, as peculiar as he is strategic, seemed seriously to overthink.

His second attempt, Little Serow, turns out to be a diminutive Thai restaurant in a disregarded, dingy basement with an unmarked entrance. Unbelievably enough, dangling light bulbs are suspended from the ceiling. The walls are haphazardly painted a shocking, abrasive shade of lime green, a crude attempt at a modern vibe. The restaurant looks like the sort of project you see when an overeager-yet-under-qualified sous chef tries to make it on his own.

It feels like it, too. The amateur staff, all previously employed by Monis, seems disconcertingly delighted when you enter—shocked, it seems, they've managed to lure you in. It may be the most overwrought welcome in the city.

One of the oddities of Komi, where diners must share the final course, is that it essentially forces strangers to dine together. Little Serow is worlds apart from most Thai restaurants, especially in that Monis does not care about serving exceptional dishes. In a very alien and un-American manner, the chef would rather serve a ceaseless, staggered meal with no flexibility. Dinner is always served as seven isolated dishes, delivered to the whole table, for a steep $45. To frustrate diners even further, the unreliable menu is changed weekly and does not permit substitutions, and the utter atmosphere of the entire meal seems more like that of a substandard neighborhood Thai joint than an exclusive restaurant.

The price is fitting for a delicate foie gras or a perfectly brazened rack of lamb. But the first course is pork rinds, an inadequate and underwhelming precursor to "larbs", a type of Thai salad completely saturated in lime dressing. The outlandish price tag is more than double what is decent for a Thai restaurant of this nature—but like a dollar store when compared to Little Serow's sister, Komi. To justify his prices, Monis uses supposedly "fresh" meats and produce.

Diners are presented with a basket of this produce, and are expected to use vegetables as substitute for traditional silverware. The sticky rice (an irritating replacement for a fork) appears for the latter half of the evening. Eating this way forces guests to stay for an excruciatingly long meal, bombarded with battling flavors and textures used as a way to soothe a blistering tongue after the initial heat wave of the scorching first dish.

The biggest inconsistency about Little Serow, besides Monis' baffling decision to branch into Thai cuisine, is the refusal to follow Western standards of portion and flavor, yet the fervor to slap a Western price tag on the meal. For $45, his "charred, hammered" beef should be a steak. Instead, Monis soaks it, slices it paper thin, and throws it in a disheveled, unappealing mass of meat on the plate. In more competent hands, the kaffir-lime-laced pork sausage would have been a succulent starting point for an exceptional dish; but the tough exterior and spongy interior of the sausage Monis prepares feels more like one it biting into human flesh than an "exotic" take on sausage.

Intensely personal undertakings such as Little Serow are often vanity projects and can be doomed. Unfortunately for Monis, his boastfully overpriced and rigid menu screams "self-indulgence." Little Serow is not about Monis' devotion to cuisine or his love of discovery, and after a never-ending seven courses over an interminable three hours, my thirst for discovery had run dry, too.

## Original (Maza, 2012)

### Smooth Sailing

With a name like Heavy Seas Alehouse, you might expect that the new bar and restaurant in Little Italy/ Harbor East would be a shrine to the esteemed Baltimore craft brewery. Hugh Sisson, the brewery's founder, said before the opening that licensing the name was meant as a showcase for the brand. And the beer list that was previewed underscored that point—all Heavy Seas, all the time.

But for all the Heavy Seas love, this isn't a venue that appeals to just fans of the beer. In fact, it is the first great new bar of the year, more than meeting the expectations set by the Heavy Seas name.

From the service to the small details in the menu, there are no false moments here. It left me wanting to come back, hoping to finally grab a glass of the Siren Noire, which wasn't available the three nights I visited, and another bite of one of the excellent burgers, available until midnight in the late night menu—a feature that will earn it many admirers in the area.

Heavy Seas Alehouse is a bar and a restaurant. Taking a big chunk of space at the Tack Factory, it's divided into three dining sections: a semiprivate area in the center, called the Captain's Lounge; an airy space near the entrance; and a third spot filled with booths and high-top tables that shares space with the bar. The bar seats about 12 and faces away from the diners and the street, giving it an intimate feel.

The decorating scheme could have been overwhelming. Patrick Dahlgren, the brains behind the bar, had promised a—shudder—nautical theme in a nod to the Heavy Seas label. I imagined something like Disney's Pirates of the Caribbean ride, with stuffed sea animals on some walls, novelty mermaids hanging from others, maybe even waiters wearing eye patches. (I'm half describing Barracudas Tavern in Locust Point.)

But Heavy Seas is spare, almost fastidious. The owners have chosen to play up the building's industrial look, and they've matched bare, exposed brick walls with colorful Heavy Seas posters that pay homage to the brand with colorful creativity…

The service is exemplary. Both bartenders and wait staff seem to be genuine fans of the place and its fare; from my stool, I could hear some recommending new beers to each other.

Heavy Seas shows a canny understanding of the young people in the neighborhood by offering a late-night menu that ends at midnight and includes an excellent Angus beef burger ($15). Order it with the Old Bay/saffron mayo on the side for the fries. The onion rings are also mouthwatering ($6.50).

In the interest of avoiding waste (and adding a neat touch), the restaurant uses the brewery's leftover spent-grain for its bread, made next door at Piedigrotta Bakery.

As for the beer, it is doubtful that there's this much Heavy Seas on display anywhere else except the brewery on the outskirts of Baltimore—two on cask and 14 on draft, including one rotating seasonal. It would be easy to scoff at the brand's monopoly, but consider the name outside, (Dogfish Head's Rehoboth Beach, Del., restaurant does the same thing.)…

The only disappointment was the staggeringly good Siren Noire, a seasonal imperial stout flavored with chocolate nibs, was not available all three nights I visited last week. It would be unfair to hold the bar responsible for being out of the Siren; bartenders told me the kegs run out quickly. In many ways, its absence speaks to Heavy Seas' huge fan base.

Reprinted with permission of The Baltimore Sun Media Group. All Rights Reserved.

# Student Rewrite
*by Lindsey Fowler:*

### Shipwrecked

With an up-front name of its product, Heavy Seas Alehouse, one would notice that this will be yet another Baltimore craft brewery. Licensing out the name of the brand by the brewery's founder, Hugh Sisson, could lead to an overexposure of the craft brewery brand. In the select preview that was available, there was a drowning amount of Heavy Seas.

The bar's expected infestation of groupies obsessed with Heavy Seas leaves little room for patrons who do not particularly like beer. While being the first bar to open this year, it's one of many bars offering what they think is the next great craft beer.

With their overwhelming attention to detail there is an OCD quality. Going back night after night, we became frustrated not to be able to order a Siren Noire, which for some inexplicable reason was out of stock.

Heavy Seas Alehouse is a bar and a restaurant. Consuming a huge amount of the Tack Factory, the many divided spaces reminded one of a broken record; a less than private area in the center of the restaurant, given the cliché name Captain's Lounge; a drafty, goose-bump-chilling space near the entrance; and a third spot jammed with booth patrons who have the unfortunate view of the backs of those sitting at the high tops and bar. The bar lacked seating, only having 12 stools, giving it a neglected feel for those facing away from the street and other diners.

The decoration was anything but overdramatic, because there was so little to see. The evil scientist behind the bar's look, Patrick Dahlgren, repeats displays of the Heavy Seas label, instead of a true authentic nautical theme.

With its lack of decoration, one would not think of the restaurant in a nautical way if the name did not give it away. The unfinished building tries to hide the fact that the walls are incomplete by blending in a mess of colors with Heavy Seas posters, again promoting the brand name.

The service could not be more robotic and by the book, appearing though the servers were filming a training video of how to treat customers. The entire staff had an almost fake appearance, pushing the patrons to try other types of beer if they were not satisfied by the one they originally ordered.

Heavy Seas finally caught onto the behavior of the younger crowd by taking advantage of the late-night, boozed-up drinkers and offering a late night menu that has $15 burgers. Along with their pricey burgers are the fries that have to be drenched in Old Bay/saffron mayo to render the taste tolerable. The onion rings are just another additional charge to the bill for added taste.

In the interest of squeezing every penny out of the restaurant, the leftover spent-grain is made into bread by the bakery next door.

The point of the bar, its beer, has an abundant amount of Heavy Seas because it is seen in so few other bars. Is this because it's a craft beer or because one must have a "craft" palate to enjoy it? One would also wonder why there is so much Heavy Seas, but what would you expect from a place named after a beer?

The restaurant seemed unprepared, as the bar ran out of Siren Noire, and couldn't replace it within the three-day visit. The only excuse was that the kegs run out fast, but wouldn't they think to overstock for an opening bar? I don't understand how they are going to keep their customers if they can't keep their product in stock.

I truly love this assignment, and so, apparently, do my students—at least those do who get passing grades on it. It has been celebrated—and not just by me—for close to four decades. It demonstrates precisely how written persuasion is effected through the use of struggle for salience-agenda and meaning-spin in opinion pieces, but the same lessons are applicable for news and "factual" journalistic coverage, just not as thoroughly.

**Persuasion Seminal Assignment Code; Frequent Words or Signs on Papers:**

**Ha!** = change so funny and clever it actually made me laugh out loud

**Good or Yes!** = perfect or nearly perfect change; superb rhetorical rework of sentence or paragraph

✓ = standard mark for a good change

**OK** = the change is acceptable, but not overly impressive **w.c.** = word choice problem: either the word you chose was inappropriate, or it made no sense in the context you used it. For some, this was a frequent problem. For some others it was a very frequent problem.

**Grade Distribution**

| A | A- | B+ | B | B- | C+ | C | C- | D | D- |
|---|----|----|---|----|----|---|----|---|----|
| 6 | 10 | 9 | 6 | 7 | 11 | 7 | 9 | 3 | 5 |

## All Decked Out
## Sanders' Corner returns to its glory days.
*by Suzanne Loudermilk*

We have a feeling this will always be Sanders' Corner. There's so much nostalgia attached to the landmark building that overlooks the Lock Raven woodshed, where generations cooled off with ice-cream cones and nibbled on old-fashioned meals, especially breakfast, in the past. But the old moniker could stick, too, because the recent name, McFaul's IronHorse Tavern at Sanders' Corner, doesn't exactly roll off the tongue. Not that it matters. What's important is that the new owners took the property and refurbished it, while still keeping old-time mementos, like the photos of the Ma and Pa Railroad trains that used to chug across the street. The spruced-up knotty-pine dining room with the A-frame ceiling and fireplace is still reminiscent of the days when the Sanders family owned the place for more than 50 years. The restaurant changed hands in 2008. But it was shuttered in early 2011, leaving its fate in question.

The new management team—W. Glen McFaul III, his wife Kristin, father-in-law Walt Lashno, and Matt Remsnyder, a co-manager at Sean Bolan's pub in Bel Air—reopened the restaurant this summer. They not only gave the place a face-lift, but they also brought in a chef who's quite capable in the kitchen.

Evan Orser, who previously worked at Looney's Pub in Bel Air and The Harp in Perry Hall, has devised an American menu that appeals to the geriatric crowd that visits during the day and the younger suburbanites, who come later for dinner, the bar scene, and music on the porch. The porch is legendary. Known for its bucolic view, it has been a mainstay at the restaurant for years. In additional to its 72 dining seats, there is now an outdoor bar to cater to the crowd. The indoor bar, featuring many local beers on tap, has been relocated to the back of the restaurant.

The chef, like many of his brethren in town, capitalizes on using local, fresh products and seafood in his preparations. The fried-green-tomatoes appetizer with local Cherry Glen goat cheese, a mound of Tilghman Island lump crab meat, and lemon-butter sauce was a fine introduction to his skills.

We also enjoyed a half-pound of steamed shrimp to start. The Old-Bay-enhanced shrimp were giant and nestled with sliced sweet potatoes (a nice touch) and onions. The portions are huge, no matter what course you're being served. The Albright Farms half-chicken—a plump bird—crackles with skin crisped with a mango-lime glaze. We got to pick our side dishes and were pleased with the whipped Yukon Gold mashed potatoes and an entree salad.

Rockfish was the featured fish of the day and was grilled perfectly, producing a moist, flaky fillet. (The fish can also be blackened.) It's paired with a fresh fruit salsa that adds a touch of sweetness and is served with wild-grain rice and asparagus.

McFaul's is also a fine place to settle in with raw-bar choices like oysters, clams, and mussels, and appetizers like Pound O'Wings, crab dip, and the chef's house-smoked fish pâté instead of succumbing to a big dinner.

Lunchtime draws diners with an array of sandwiches, pizza, soups, and salads (all offered at dinner, too). The salmon BLT was piled high with a six-ounce fillet, applewood-smoked bacon, lettuce, and tomato on a ciabatta roll. The Iron "Power" House was a great version of the veggie favorite with lettuce, tomato, sprouts, cucumbers, carrots, avocado, cheese, and hummus on multi-grain bread.

Desserts are really good here, too. Besides local Prigel ice cream, Sanders' Corner—oops, McFaul's— offers selections made by Baltimore bakery Sasscer's Cheesecake. We had a slice of the three-layer carrot cake with the right amount of cream-cheese icing and a cheesecake blanketed with a berry compote.

We would have been happy just to sit on the porch and gaze at the treetops when we heard the restaurant has reopened. And we'll do that. But we're also looking forward to returning and enjoying the bounty from the kitchen as well.

**McFaul's Ironhorse Tavern At Sanders Corner:** *2260 Cromwell Bridge Rd., 410-828-1625* **HOURS** *11 a.m.-12 a.m. Sun.-Wed., 11 a.m.-1 a.m. Thurs.-Sat.; brunch, 10 a.m.-2 p.m. Sat.-Sun.* **CUISINE** *American* **PRICE** *Appetizers: $6-14; entrees $12-33; sandwiches: $5-14; desserts: $5-7.* **ATMOSPHERE**: *Casual with nostalgic dining rooms, a lively bar area, and a great porch overlooking Loch Raven watershed.*

Reprinted with permission of Baltimore magazine, Oct. 2012.

## Student Rewrite
*by Garrett Levy*

✓

## Faults at McFaul's

Sanders' Corner is a thing of the past.

good

The restaurant, once known as Sanders' Corner, is facing a bit of an identity crisis.

✓

Though the building still overlooks the Loch Raven woodshed, it lacks the idyllic

✓

atmosphere it once had. The latest name, McFaul's IronHorse Tavern at Sander's

✓            yes

Corner, is quite a mouthful. Like the restaurant itself, the name could certainly use

another change. The restaurant still has the photos of the local Ma and Pa Railroad

✓

trains, but ever since its renovation by the new owners, the restaurant has forfeited

good word choice

some of its nostalgic vibe. The antiquated fireplace and archaic A-frame ceiling are

✓                    ✓

still holding up, but who knows how much longer they will last? In 2008, the new

owners stepped in, looking to alter the beloved local restaurant. Then in 2011, the

abruptly                    ✓

restaurant was closed down, leaving customers in the dark.

In an attempt to meet the desires of both the older and younger crowds, the new

✓

chef, Evan Orser, has settled for a plain American menu. The aging porch actually

✓

used to be the highlight of the whole place. The atmosphere and view from the porch

✓

were peaceful at times, but the addition of a noisy outdoor bar detracted from the

✓                    ✓

feeling of serenity. With only 72 seats for dining, the bar area can become congested

✓

rather quickly on a busy day. The indoor bar, which now hides in the back of the

✓

restaurant, features only local beers on tap.

*just great subtlety in your negative review*

The cook uses plain ingredients commonly used by other chefs in the area. The

✓

fried-green-tomatoes appetizer that he eventually served was covered with a peculiar

✓

goat cheese, some crab-meat, and an intense lemon-butter sauce.

added fact                    ✓

Next was a messy half-pound of steamed shrimp. For some reason, the shrimp,

loaded with Old Bay, were paired with onions and sweet potatoes.

✓                    ✓

Regardless of which course it was, the portion sizes remained the same. A strange

mango-lime concoction coated the half-chicken from Albright Farms. A simple salad

ha!

and a serving of yellowish mashed potatoes were provided with the meal. The only

good re-emphasis

options available for the fish of the day, Rockfish, were grilled and blackened. The

yes, yes

odd combination with fruit salsa gave it an unexpected sweetness, conflicting with

the wild-grain rice and side of asparagus.

*very good*

## A Sanders Corner without the Sanders family just isn't quite the same.

McFaul's offers alternatives like seafood oversized appetizers in case the conventional

✓                                                                    ✓

entrees become too tiresome. The restaurant offers a lot of the same basic foods for

✓

lunch and dinner. The cook threw together a salmon BLT sandwich made with just a

✓

six-ounce fillet. The Iron "Power" House, a strictly veggie-filled sandwich on multi-

✓

grain bread, lacks substance and tastes just as bland as it sounds.

✓

If any stomach space was still available, the standard desserts might have been

✓

more desirable. Despite having a capable chef, McFaul's seems to rely on other

✓

businesses to make the desserts they serve. The slices of cheesecake and carrot cake

might                                                      *good*

~~would~~ have tasted fresher if McFaul's didn't outsource their desserts.

At first, it was exciting to hear Sanders' Corner had reopened, but with the new

✓                          ✓

management and modifications it just doesn't feel the same. The nostalgic vibes *excellent last line*

must have departed along with the Sanders family. At least there's still a decent view.

*This is so good and rhetorically sophisticated; you reverse it, yet keep the professionalism of a serious critic. Really just a superb rewrite—you are a natural rhetorician.*

*May I have a zeroxed copy of the rewrite (with my comments) + original at your convenience?*

## A Touch of Victorian Grace on the Delaware Shore

*by Zofia Smardz,*
*Sep 30, 2012 06:40 PM EDT*

The Washington Post: September 30, 2012

*A biweekly staff review of East Coast and regional lodgings.*

You don't like tchotchkes? Or doilies? No fusty fringy boudoir-style lampshades for you? Hmm. Then you probably won't like the Boardwalk Plaza Hotel.

But then again—trust me here—you may. You really, really may. In fact, I'm sure you will.

I base my faith in this on a simple observation. On a recent evening, my husband and I are nursing some drinks at the bar of the hotel on the boardwalk at Rehoboth Beach, Del. As dusk slowly descends over the swaying sea grasses and the ocean waves, we observe the number of people who walk past the graceful pink and white lady and screech to a halt before the old-timey photo board that stands out front: you know, a board painted with life-size figures in old fashioned Victorian dress, with holes where the heads should be. If I'd had a dollar for every person who poked their noggin through one of those head holes, like a penitent in a pillory, to pose for a snapshot as a Victorian matron on patriarch at the shore…Well, I'd have had enough for several rounds of drinks. At least.

There's just something about the idea of Victorians at the beach, you know?

Tromping over the sand dunes in their high-button regalia—it's so funny. And yet, credit where it's due: They were the ones who popularized the beach as a leisure destination. In fact, as marketing director Jennifer Zerby reminds us in a video clip on the hotel web site, Rehoboth itself has Victorian roots: It was founded in 1873 as a Methodist meeting camp. So think of the 84-room Boardwalk Plaza as a sort of tribute to the era. And one that capitalizes on its legacy simply, uh, capitally.

Just come on into the lobby with me. The lights are soothingly low, as in a Victorian drawing room—fringy lamps, don't you know, and those big double-barreled glass ones—the woodwork dark and the walls papered. The sofas are the real thing, all high, curvy back and thick arms and dark, shiny fabrics. Or velvet, of course. A gorgeous floral centerpiece crowns the scarf-covered table in the center. And what's this lying beside it? Why, a genuine stereopticon! Let's have a peek. Oh, such old-fashioned amusement.

But wait, here's something even better. Birds! Nothing more Victorian than a parrot or two, squawking a noisy welcome. Well, one of them squawks. The big gray one sits quietly, but the brilliant, rainbow-colored bird in the cage by the lobby's marble fireplace is a truly noisy fellow. I ask the front desk clerk what type he is. "A sun conyer," she says. (At least that's what I think she says. I look it up later—ah, a sun conure, a variety of South American parakeet. Live and learn.) I'm tempted to coax it onto my finger, but then I read the sign that says the birds could bite, so do it at your own risk. Never mind.

Let's move on, and you'll see that for all the period atmosphere and decor, there's nothing fusty or musty about the Boardwalk Plaza. Even into its third decade (it opened in 1991), the hotel looks pretty and feels fresh, which is astounding for a beach property, if you ask me. The carpeting looks as if it had been laid yesterday; I spy not a speck of sand en route to our room. Amazing.

Our two-room ocean-view suite is large and comfortable, and—oh, I didn't expect this—it sports a spiffy kitchenette! There's a microwave and a range and a toaster and, of course, a one-cup Keurig coffeemaker. Wish we were staying for a week. As it is, the coffeemaker will get a workout, between the two of us.

The decor here is more faux than in the lobby, but I have to tell you—after all the monochromatic hotel rooms with their blinding white bedding, the sight of the floral comforters on the queen beds fills me with a pleasant nostalgia.

As does the three-level dining room, with its flowered carpeting and white tableclothes and the ornamental fretwork around the large windows that look out upon the ocean, like in a ship's dining room. As we wait for our meals to arrive, I finger the little bell on the table, wondering what would happen if I rang it. Of course I don't, but later, as I'm tucking into the filet (exquisite), the woman one table over inadvertently does. Next thing I know, the hostess is at my side saying, "How may I help you, madam?"

"Oh it wasn't me," I laugh, but I'm impressed.

After dinner, we take a stroll onto the boardwalk, where the post-season crowds are much thinner, the air cooler, the concession lights somewhat fewer. But outside the Boardwalk Plaza, one thing hasn't changed. Over at the photo board, someone's just poked his head through a hole for a snapshot.

**Boardwalk Plaza Hotel**
2 Olive Ave. and the Boardwalk Rehoboth Beach, Del.
800-332-3224
www.boardwalkplaza.com

Open year-round. Off-season rates for 2012: Aug. 31-Oct. 7 from $184; Oct. 8-20 from $154; Oct. 21 to Nov. 24 from $94; Nov. 25-Dec. 31 from $79.

## Student Rewrite
*By Emily Brient*

✓

A Victorian Disaster on the Delaware Shore

✓

If you're anything like me, you'd say, what's with all the tchotchkes? And those unnecessary
✓

ornamental mats? Not into high fashion, outdated, ancient French style furnishings? I'm
✓        ✓       ✓

not surprised. The distasteful Boardwalk Plaza is all of these things, plus many more.
✓

It only took but one glimpse for me to notice that the flavorless decor has fallen flat. The
✓

only way to cure the dissatisfaction was to down some drinks at the hotel bar overlooking
✓

the boardwalk at Rehoboth Beach, Delaware. As we were waiting for this day finally to
✓

end, the sun couldn't sink fast enough while we gawked at the people who strolled past
✓

the Pepto-Bismol pink and white building as the outdated photo board practically jumped
✓

out at them: yeah, those corny boards painted with life size people in unstylish Victorian
✓       ✓

dresses, with holes where some actually dare to put their head through. If I had a dollar for

every bonehead who poked their absent-minded skull through those tacky holes…Well, I

would have enough money for plenty more, much needed cocktails. If only I could have

been so lucky.    so far, right on the mark—flows well, believable

Let us start with the lobby. The lights are so dim that it's hard to see anything, but <u>who</u>   } good

<u>could miss the tasteless, double-barreled</u> glass fringy lamps, the gloomy woodwork and
✓

the wallpaper that seems to be tearing from the walls? The sofas couldn't look more out of
✓

place; they are overstated with their curvy back, thick arms, and tacky black leather. I think
✓

it's leather anyway, although it could be faux along with the rest of the décor. A poorly-
✓

thrown-together floral centerpiece is a distraction from the dreadful tablecloth it's sitting
✓

on. And what's lying beside it? A stereopticon—I didn't think people actually used those

anymore. This just adds to the amusement.

this is really excellent so far—exactly what I'm looking for

The atmosphere is nothing less than fusty-dusty. I'm in disbelief that the Boardwalk } good, and it's almost all good

✓          ✓

Plaza has made it to its third decade, seeing that it looks like it has taken a beating over the

✓

years. The carpet, which I assume was once white, is surely not up to my standards as I

would consider it an offsetting brown; I'm surprised I'm not getting sand stuck to my feet

✓                    ✓

as I'm walking through the halls. Unbelievable.

pretentious                              ✓

Our two-room flat was enormous and overly ~~prestigious~~—I was excited for a second—

✓                                        ✓

when I saw a miniature kitchen. Don't get your hopes up; there's a small department-store-

✓              yes!

bought microwave, an outdated range, an ancient toaster and, even worse, one of those

trendy, useless, one-cup Keurig coffeemakers. We'd sure be in trouble if we were trapped

yes!

here for a week. The wanna-be coffeemaker will get a workout considering it only makes

one dinky copy of coffee at a time.

✓          ✓

If possible, the décor up here is more faux than the rest of the place, but I never thought I'd

say this—I now prefer all the monochromatic hotel rooms to these pastel floral comforters

✓

that honestly sicken me.

After what seems like the most dreadful day I've ever had on a vacation, we walked along

the boardwalk in desperate need to get away from the Boardwalk Plaza. I'm somehow not

✓

surprised to see that one thing hasn't changed. I notice someone's still getting a kick out of

that childlike photo board.

What an extraordinarily excellent rewrite! Your rhetorical talent is evident throughout.
Exquisitely creative, plausible, well-written changes: one of the papers ever.
May I have zeroxed copy of this rewrite and the original at your convenience?

# A Beethoven Quartet, Better Heard Than Seen
*by Alastair Macaulay*

The systematic dreariness of D. D. Dorvillier's "Danza Permanente" is depressing—schematic and soporific. In the first place, the ambience onstage is disagreeable. Four dancers metronomically plod their way through long routines, occasionally counting out loud. Usually they avert their eyes from one another and the audience—but sometimes they connect conspiratorially, like prisoners who are hoping the guards will not notice their escape plan. The escape, of course, came when they stopped.

One of the four dancers, Nuno Bizarro, will be 50 in 2014, according to a program note. Another, Walter Dunderville, looks older, with his gray beard and shaven skull. They're not too old to execute their movement, but they bring it no bloom, no juice; and the dance texture throughout feels meager. All four dancers wear twin sets of long-sleeved shirts and short shorts, each in a different color. At the start they all wear jazz shoes, which some later remove for subsequent section of this four-part piece. Some thigh muscles look less equal than others.

*   *   *

Ms. Dorvillier, the choreographer, writes in a program note that "Danza Permanente" is her attempt to make music visible in silence; the music is one of Beethoven's sublime late string quartets, Opus 132 in A minor ("Heiliger Dankesang"). The quartet would challenge even the greatest choreographers. There are good reasons that few Beethoven dances have stayed in repertory: despite their dance rhythms, Beethoven's constructions resist the structures of formal choreography.

## Beethoven Quartet: Audibly and Visibly Pleasing

*Isobel Kuckinsky*

D.D. Dorvillier's "Danza Permanente" offers consistent entertainment that is emotional, thoughtful and attention-seeking. To begin, the onstage presence is simple, yet inspiring. The four performers rhythmically execute their routines, counting out loud to further indulge the audience. There are moments when the dancers withdraw to themselves for inspiration, but when they do connect with each other—and then the audience—the result is powerful. Once the dancing stops, the audience wants more.

The program notes that dancer Nuno Bizarro, will be celebrating his 50th birthday in 2014. Another dancer, Walter Dunderville, shows his experience and age with a shaven head and distinguished gray facial hair. Their maturity brings a sense of carefulness, appreciation and love to the movements, giving the dance passion. Wearing similarly long sleeved shirts, the dancers stand together while the difference in color of their shorts boldly sets them apart. Although the dancers all begin by wearing jazz shoes, the four-part piece give them a chance to dance more naturally by their removing their shoes. This in turn shows the diversity of each dancer's build.

Dorvillier states that by using "Heiliger Dankgesang" (a string quartet in A minor) for her piece "Danza Permanente," she will successfully show how music can be visible, even in silence. Even world-renowned choreographers would see the reward in this challenging quartet. Beethoven's music often has challenged choreographers to overcome its structural restrictions and create exemplary pieces that will stay circulating in the dance world.

## Kit Wascom Pollard, "Good Time, Good Food," The Baltimore Sun, March 9, 2014:

The kitchen, led by Daniel Chaustit, the former owner of now-closed Crush in Belvedere Square, gets the job done. A simple chip-and-dip snack was better than expected, thanks to warm, ruffled chips and thick, well-seasoned dip. Beef-filled empanadas, served with a spicy red pepper sauce, were savory and steamy.

Chorizo and bread crumb-stuffed clams, Lib's take on clams casino, were toasty, salty, and just spicy enough. Cooked until the clams were hot, but still plump, they were one of our favorite dishes.

"Good time and good food at Lib's Grill in Perry Hall" by K. Pollard. First published in *The Baltimore Sun*, March 7, 2014.

## Student Rewrite

*by Shawn Greenwald*

### Bad Times; Worse Food

The kitchen was led by Daniel Chaustit, the former owner of the unsuccessful and out-of-business Crush in Belvedere Square. The unmistakable chip-and-dip snack was remarkably a recipe filled with mistakes, thanks to lukewarm, disheveled chips and overly-seasoned dip. The empanadas were packed with so much beef that it overwhelms the dish. It did not help that the dish was drenched in an oil-sogged liquid they misleadingly called "spicy red pepper sauce."

Lib's uniquely bad interpretation of clams casino, the Chorizo and crumb-stuffed clams, might have been tolerable if it hadn't been for the excessive salts and spices. The clams were overcooked and were one of our least favorite dishes among a host of other bad ones.

\* \* \*

*The Washington Post*, Anne Midgette's 'Moby-Dick' sails on a tuneful Sea?", February 23, 2014.

## Original

If you like traditional opera, you will probably like "Moby-Dick." Hegie and Scheer have hewn to operatic models that work. Their opera features big tunes for full orchestra, impassioned arias and tender ensembles, and choral scenes for sailors yo-ho-hoing as they tug at ropes on the foredeck.

In an operatic landscape crowded with various noteworthy reinventions of the wheel that have not managed to travel very far, Moby-Dick is eminently drivable.

## Student Rewrite

*Nina Glose*

### "Moby Dick" Capsizes Under Unpleasant Tides

If you enjoy operas that are without modification and are attached-at-the-hip to its traditions, then I suppose this is the opera for you. Heggie and Scheer try to follow tried-and-true operatic models, but they just don't work. Their opera features gaudy tunes for its overly-crowded orchestra, overly melodramatic arias (that sound eerily similar to a hormonal teenager) coupled with a feeble ensemble, and cliched choral scenes of sailors rowdily yo-ho-hoing as they affectedly tug at ropes on a foredeck. Although various proverbial reinventions of the wheel have not traveled very far in the opera world, think about this: at least they traveled. "Moby Dick seems to be traveling all right: to the ocean floor!"

## Original
*By David Hochman*

"Peak Vermont" August/September 2019

Vermont in summer is a breezy pleaser if you do it right. On an extended weekend, the Green Mountain State lives up to its billing, with endless possibilities in those pine-colored hills and a rare sense that getting the most from a place sometimes involves taking it easy. Cell service isn't a guarantee in the woodsier spots, which describes much of Vermont, so it's fine to ditch the devices and pick blueberries or perhaps some black-eyed Susans instead. And because average temperatures hover around 70 and daylight lingers past 9 pm, summer tends to over-deliver in these parts.

## Student Rewrite

Teresa Barnaba

Changed from positive to negative

### Unremarkable Vermont

Vermont's summers are irritatingly windy if you don't plan accordingly. If you stay for a long weekend, you'll wonder if the Green Mountain State truly has anything to offer, as there is little to do except stare at the endless rows of pine trees. Not to mention that guests can't even receive cell service, an unfortunate feature of Vermont, so guests are left to either twiddle their thumbs or pick through the brush. And don't plan on enjoying cool nights or getting well-deserved rest. The temperature is a painstakingly 70 degrees and the sun doesn't set until well past 9 pm, leaving summer to linger around like an annoying younger sibling.

## Original

*By Bryan Alexander*
USA Today

*"Rambo Keeps Kills Feeling Fresh"*

Fans who like vengeful gore get plenty of it

"First Blood" famously saw one small-town lawman who beat Rambo take a spiked spring trap to the legs. The gore, and deaths, have been amplified throughout subsequent films. "Last Blood" includes an unflinching scene of a high-ballistic bullet to a foe's face.

"It's horrifying, but I don't want to fake it," Stallone said at a news conference last week. "When it's a Rambo film, they expect to be uncomfortable when it gets to the killing fields."

Nothing is deemed too gory. Director Adrian Grunberg recalls one scene where Rambo sprays bullets into cartel combatants already dying in pain. The moment was temporarily cut.

"And then it was like, 'Rambo hates them. He wants to spit on their graves,'" Grunberg tells USA TODAY. "So we put that back in."

## Student Rewrite

Tiffany James

Positive to Negative

*ha!*    **'Rambo' Kills Need to Die Already**   *GOOD!*

**Fans who delight in gratuitous violence will be happy**

"First Blood" satisfied viewers by shredding an enemy's legs in a spiked spring trap. Modern fans require more gore to satisfy their bloodlust. "Last Blood" serves up a gut-wrenching viewing of a foe's face destroyed by a high-ballistic bullet.

*yes!*

"It's horrifying," Stallone admitted during a news conference. "When it's a Rambo film, they expect to be uncomfortable."

The gore crosses the line. Director Adrian Grunberg originally cut a scene where Rambo unnecessarily annihilates a dying group of foes, but Grunberg succumbed and put it back in against his better judgment.

"I know it's Rambo," one moviegoer said, "but that last scene nearly made me sick." *good*

## Works Cited

Bitzer, Lloyd F. (1968). The Rhetorical Situation. *Philosophy and Rhetoric*, 1:1-14.

Gorelick, Richard. (September 26, 2010). "Authentic Flavors of Milan." *The Baltimore Sun*. 8.

Kliman, Todd. (February 2012). High on Thai. *The Washingtonian*. 120-121.

Large, Elizabeth. (March 7, 2004). Going to XS is, well, fun. *The Baltimore Sun*. 8N. Loudermilk, Suzanne. (October 2012). "All Decked Out," *Baltimore Magazine*, 182-183. Macaulay, Alastair. (September 2, 2012) "A Beethoven Quartet, Better Heard Than Seen." *The New York Times*.

Maza, Eric. (March 2, 2012). Smooth Sailing. *The Baltimore Sun*. 15.

Smardz, Zofia. (September 30, 2012). "A touch of Victorian Grace on the Delaware Shore," *The Washington Post*, F4.

Vatz, Richard E. (1973). The myth of the rhetorical situation. *Philosophy and Rhetoric*. 6: 154-161.

# Heartbreak Revisited

### In 'A Star Is Born,' an old-fashioned belief in big-feeling cinema comes through.

"A STAR IS BORN" is such a great Hollywood myth that it's no wonder Hollywood keeps telling it. Whatever the era, the director or the headliners, it relates the story of two lovers on dramatically differing paths: a famous man who's furiously racing to the bottom (Bradley Cooper in this movie) and a woman (Lady Gaga) who's soaring to the top. This latest and fourth version is a gorgeous heartbreaker (bring tissues). Like its

*✓ A Star Is Born*
*Directed by Bradley Cooper*

Lady Gaga and Bradley Cooper, who also directed, has gone all in with big emotions and cascades of tears.

finest antecedents, it wrings tears from its romance and thrills from a steadfast belief in old-fashioned, big-feeling cinema. That it's also a perverse fantasy about men, women, love and sacrifice makes it all the better.

Like the last iteration, the epically (empirically!) terrible 1976 remake with Barbra Streisand and Kris Kristofferson, the new one is set in a contemporary music world that is by turns exciting, suffocating and

crowded with dangers — ravenous fans, crushing performance demands, celebrity itself. This is the world that has helped create and come close to ruining Jackson Maine (Mr. Cooper), a country-rock musician who, when the movie opens, is performing obviously wasted, leaning and nearly falling into a boot-stomping song. He's a beautiful ruin adrift on an ocean of booze, one he routinely spikes with pills.

CONTINUED ON PAGE C9

*[handwritten: Tyler Williams]*

*[handwritten: actually I chose to keep this line]*

*[handwritten: No horizontal lines!!!!]*

## 25 Win 'Genius' Grants

MacArthur fellowships go to writers, scientists, artists and a human rights lawyer.

By SOPAN DEB

There was laundry to be done for Okwui Okpokwasili, a choreographer and performer, as she walked out of her Brooklyn home early last month toward a laundromat. She was getting ready to fly to Berlin that night and, to her irritation, she kept missing calls from an unidentified number. When Ms. Okpokwasili, 46, returned the call, an automated voice message provided no clarity. Maybe she was getting spammed, she thought. Then her phone rang again showing the same number and

spamming tone.' So I dialed back my aggroness," Ms. Okpokwasili said.

The man had been trying to get in touch to tell her she was receiving one of this year's 25 John D. and Catherine T. MacArthur Foundation fellowships. Commonly if not officially known as "genius" grants, they recognize "exceptional creativity" in various fields and come with no-strings-attached awards of $625,000 each, distributed over five years.

The selection process, and the people who choose the winners, are kept mostly confidential, but 20 to 30 fellows are picked every year, with the hope that the money and recognition will help spur more creative work. There are no applications for the award. Past winners include Lin-Manuel Miranda and David Simon, but most of the

## A Teena Discover Her Pur

In 'The Hate Give,' the dea friend at the a cop pushes young woma to take a stan Review, Page

MANOHLA DARGIS | FILM REVIEW

# A Gorgeous Heartbreak Revisited

CONTINUED FROM PAGE C1

A singer with a voice that can thunder, Ally Campana (Lady Gaga) becomes Jack's safe harbor, taking on the roles of lover, partner, muse, ideal. That's a heavy burden, but Ally is one of life's chin-up survivors, with an errant mother and a loving, larger-than-life father, Lorenzo (a terrific Andrew Dice Clay), whose dreams cloud her own. Dad runs a limo business out of their Los Angeles home, where his male colleagues (Barry Shabaka Henley, among others) and their boisterous camaraderie fill the rooms, both warming and crowding them. Ally is accustomed to navigating around men larger than she is, elbowing past them to be seen and heard.

She and Jack first meet late one night in a Hollywood drag club where she sings after her waitress shift ends. Jack has just finished playing a concert and, after polishing off a bottle of booze, has stumbled into the club for more. There he watches Ally belt out the Edith Piaf standard "La Vie en Rose," in a sheath and upsweep, her arched artificial brows adding quizzical punctuation to her face. In a swoon, he invites her out that night, and, as flirtation gives way to deeper feelings, they fall in love. He brings Ally onstage and then on tour, but she eventually goes solo, becoming a star whose ascent is shadowed by his decline.

Mr. Cooper, who also directed, does a lot right in this take on "A Star Is Born," beginning with the casting of Lady Gaga, whose disarming, naturalistic presence is crucial to the movie's force. A post-Madonna pop artist known for her elaborate stagecraft and costumes, she has been stripped down here, her mask removed. You can see her skin, the flutter in her veins, which brings you close to her, and can make both the actress and her character feel touchingly vulnerable. This unmasking of Lady Gaga also makes Ally seem genuine, authentic, a quality that the movie champions and that serves as a kind of thematic first principle.

Soon after Jack and Ally meet, he peels off one of her fake brows — he's flirting, but he's also saying that he sees the real her and wants the world to as well. Playful yet unapologetically earnest, this scene inaugurates a seduction — of Ally, of us — that lasts the exhilarating first hour. Mr. Cooper understands the power of big-screen myths, including thunderstruck love and near-magical lucky breaks. He also understands his own star appeal (he gives himself plenty of heat-stoking close-ups), which dovetails with his role as director. When Ally and Jack look at each other, you're watching two people fall in love, and it's a contact high. You're also watching a director guiding — creating — his star as life seeps into fiction.

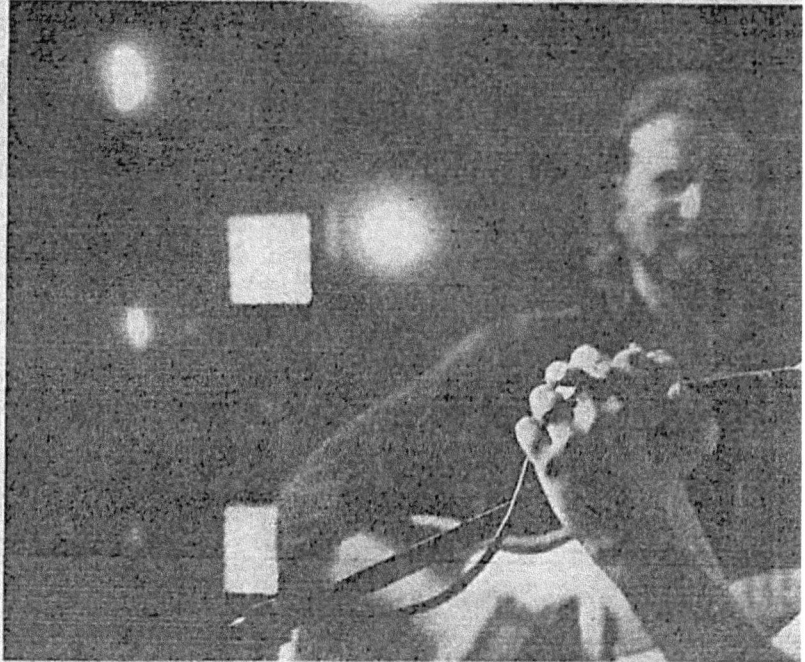

Mr. Cooper's smartest decision, other than casting Lady Gaga, is the absolute sincerity with which he's taken on this material, in all its gorgeous, gaudy excess. He has refurbished the story some and added a bit too much psychological filler, but he has stayed true to its fundamental seriousness. Winking at this story would have been easy, but would have destroyed it. Instead, working from a script he wrote with Eric Roth and Will Fetters, Mr. Cooper has gone all in

## Giving a defining Hollywood tale the polish and scale it merits.

with big emotions and cascades of tears. (The movie owes a debt to, and nods at, the original 1937 film as well as the 1954 remake with a peerless Judy Garland.)

Part of what's exciting about this "A Star Is Born" is that Mr. Cooper knows he's telling one of the defining Hollywood stories and has given the movie the polish and scale it merits. He plays with intimacy and cinematic sweep, going in close when Ally and Jack are together, so that the world falls away — a scene of them in a parking lot shows how conversation turns to courtship — only to then pull back so we can see the enormity of the world the lovers inhabit once Jack takes Ally on tour. And while the crowd seems little more than a surging blur the first time Jack plays, when Ally looks at the throng, she sees it and so do we.

The concert scenes of Jack and Ally performing are revved up but personal. (The production borrowed crowds from actual music festivals like Coachella, and their sheer size conveys the scope of Jack's stardom.) Mr. Cooper sings pleasantly enough and throttles an electric guitar with persuasive fervor. He's backed by the group Lukas Nelson & the Promise of the Real (Lukas's dad is Willie Nelson). The music mixes standards with new songs, some written by Mr. Cooper, Lukas Nelson and Lady Gaga, whose supple, often electric singing can, at full throttle, express intensities of feeling far better than the dialogue.

Like many filmmakers, Mr. Cooper sometimes explains too much. It isn't enough that Jack drinks; Mr. Cooper wants us to know why. So he fleshes out Jack's past, turning melodrama into therapy and robbing the character of mystery. One of the weakest scenes, a violent confrontation between Jack and his much-older brother, Bobby (Sam Elliott, whose deep drawl Mr. Cooper has borrowed), is an information dump. In one of the finest, Bobby just wordlessly drives away from Jack, and Mr. Elliott lets you see the ferocity of the brothers' love — and their pain — in eyes that have begun

Tyler Williams

WARNER BROS. PICTURES

Bradley Cooper and Lady ~~Gaga in "A Star Is Born."~~ ~~he character he plays is~~ ~~damaged, hers is insecure.~~

**✓ A Star Is Born**

CRITIC'S PICK

Rated R for alcohol and drug abuse, and some physical violence. Running time: 2 hours 15 minutes.

*No horizontal line!*

to ~~water and in a stone face that will shatter.~~ Mr. Cooper spends more time on the story's male lead than previous iterations have, perhaps because he's taken the role himself. The focus on Jack — he scrapes bottom, goes into recovery — somewhat weighs down the remainder of the movie, partly because too much of it is overly familiar. At times, Mr. Cooper seems to share Jack's unease with Ally's stardom, particularly after she connects with a manager (Rafi Gavron, oozing sleaze) and transforms from a soulful crooner into a writhing automaton with soulless beats and backup singers. Ally puts on the mask that Mr. Cooper has removed from Lady Gaga, suggesting that — unlike Jack's — her art is less than pure.

Male self-aggrandizement is baked into the story's foundation but not ruinously. ~~Jack doesn't just help turn Ally into a star, giving her the big break she needs. His trauma — she's insecure, but he's damaged — becomes a deep well that she draws from, allowing her to become a greater artist. In~~ part, the story is as creaky as that of Pygmalion, ~~the male~~ sculptor who turns a beloved carving into a woman. Yet one of the pleasures of "A Star Is Born" in all its renditions is that it is also about a woman whose ambitions are equal to those of any man and who steadily rises as she weeps and sings toward fabulous self and sovereignty.

## Tyler Williams
*word count: 499*

✓

'A Star Is Born' Serves Deja Vu and Heartburn

✓

'A Star Is Born' is such a cash cow that it's no wonder Hollywood continues to

✓ ✓

grind it up and spit it back out. Every time, it stutters over the tale of two lovers on

✓ ✓

predictable paths: famous man who's pitifully racing to the bottom (Bradley Cooper)

✓ ✓

and a woman (Lady Gaga) who's naively soaring to the top. This attempt is a milque-

ha!

toast snore-fest (bring coffee, or, even better, a pillow). The only tears the audience

✓ ✓

will shed this time come from the film's unfiltered awkwardness and outdated tropes.

✓

Like the miserable 1976 remake with Barbra Streisand and Kris Kristofferson,

✓

the film struggles to simulate today's glitzy music world, scribbling a portrait of

✓ ✓

an industry that seems claustrophobic, soul-eating and chock-full of regret. This is

✓ ✓

the world that unconvincingly built-up–and broke down—Jackson Maine (Cooper),

✓

a country-rock musician. When the movie opens, Jack is performing (excessively)

wasted, leaning and nearly falling into a boot-stomping song, yet it's hard to tell how

✓ ✓ ha! great!

much of the act is Jack's character or Cooper's clumsiness.

✓ ✓

Cooper, who thought he could have his cake and eat it too, missteps in almost

✓

every conceivable way as a director, beginning with the casting of Lady Gaga, whose

✓ ✓

half-baked, unrefined presence is as smart as Silicon Valley's "raw water" trend. A

✓ ✓

Madonna wannabe, known for her meat-suits and pubescent anthems, Gaga ditches

the persona that made her famous, and viewers can't help but wish she'd put her

✓ yes ✓ ✓

mask back on. Her uncharacteristic change of pace matches her portrayal of Ally:

✓

out of place, uncomfortable, and something no one asked for—a disadvantage from

✓

which the film cannot recover.     this is so good, so far

✓

Cooper, known for the Hangover series, is no stranger to Hollywood flops; he

✓

struggles to rekindle the themes of luck and love the original half-decently conveyed.

✓

His narcissism seeps onto the big screen (he greedily inserted plenty of his own

✓                                                                                                    ha!

grimace-inducing close-ups), suggesting that he should've stuck to voicing humanoid

Raccoons for Marvel. When Ally and Jack look at each other, all you'll be looking

✓

for is the exit door and Pepto.

good

Jack's backstory is a dead horse that Cooper beats so hard it looks like it belongs

✓

in his beloved American Sniper. It isn't enough that Jack drinks; Bradley insists

we know why. So, he delivers a sequence that reminiscent of the flashback disco

clever ✓                                        ✓

scene in *Airplane!*, except this time the prolonged sequence isn't funny. The absolute

weakest scene, a violent confrontation between Jack and his brother, Bobby (Sam

✓

Elliott, whose accent Cooper steals), lost any chance of emotional resonance when

✓                          ✓

it developed into an info dump.

✓

Unsurprisingly, Cooper stained the film with a heaping dose of male self-

aggrandizement. He denies the viewers of the greatest pleasure of any passable "A

Star Is Born" archetype. Instead, he sloppily offers a woman whose ambitions equate

ha!

to something from a Barbie doll box and who submerges a drowning man to push

✓

herself closer to a mirage of fabulous self and sovereignty.

For the most part, a brilliant rewrite, clever, plausible & compelling.
May I have a copy of the xeroxed copy of the rewrite + original at your convenience?

## Original
**NR PLUS FILM & TV**
*The Batman Smells*
**By Jack Butler**

The rest of the cast is talented, but mostly wasted. Jeffrey Wright is adequate as Batman's police ally Jim Gordon, though he at times tries a little too hard to seem like a grizzled veteran of the force. Colin Farrell is pointlessly unrecognizable as Italian-gangster caricature the Penguin. Zoë Kravitz is uninteresting as—let's just say it—Catwoman, who has nothing of Michelle Pfeiffer's allure or ambiguity and gets trapped in a couple of subplots to give her something to do. Andy Serkis is barely present as trusted butler Alfred—who, by the way, actually is *not* that trusted by Bruce Wayne, who keeps him at arm's length. That about rounds out the major cast.

They fill a movie that is far too long, with a story that seems complex but is mostly just dragged out. It turns on a mélange of the same themes that live-action incarnations of the character have been working with since Burton: Gotham is corrupt, Gotham's elite is corrupt, is Batman the same as the villains he fights, can the city be saved, is Batman a symbol, etc. But what made *The Batman* particularly frustrating was a weird refusal to go all-in on any one of these themes, leaving me with just aftertastes of better-executed examples in prior films, and its abiding atmosphere of dark-dark-darkness.

## Student Rewrite

*The Batman Exhilarates*
By Hollyn Bush

The rest of the cast is a powerful ✔ collection of talent. Jeffrey Wright as Batman's fearless confidant Jim Gordon, brilliantly ✔ executes his role as an experienced ✔ leader of the police force. Colin Farrell perfectly ✔ embodies the persona of one of Batman's most famous nemeses [**GOOD PLURAL**), Italian-gangster Penguin. Zoe Kravitz stuns and ✔ captivates the audience as Catwoman, with the ✔ same enchantment and ✔ elegance as Michelle Pfeiffer, while keeping viewers invested in her every move throughout the film. Andy Serkis takes on the honor ✔ and responsibility of representing Bruce Wayne's most trusted advisor and mentor Alfred, with whom he entrusts his life. ✔

Time was clearly well spent illustrating ✔ the chronicle of The Batman. A timeless tribute to the immortal ✔ Batman story: Gotham counting on ✔

Batman to save the city, Batman, a hero, defeating villains—mentally and physically—time and time again ✔ , proving himself as an everlasting [**yes**] symbol ✔ of hope for Gotham: a satisfying blend ✔ of these themes is what creates the classic familiarity ✔ that is The Batman. The audience is left wanting more of the shadowed yet mysterious atmosphere. ✔ **[THIS IS VERY IMPRESSIVE]**

## Original

Original: from *Wall Street Journal* April 14, 2022
Fantastic Beasts
By Joe Morgenstern

It's a genuine mystery. Productions can go wrong. Certain elements can fail to ignite or cohere. Bad stuff happens all the time, especially in industrial enterprises of this magnitude, but usually there's some good stuff to dilute the debacle. Not here, though.

The original idea was questionable: Go back to J.K. Rowling's fountain of revenue—and enchantment—by summoning up the Harry Potter universe before Harry. It worked well enough in 2016 for the first film out of the ornate new gate, "Fantastic Beasts and Where to Find Them," but not well all two years later in "Fantastic Beasts: The Crimes of Grindelwald."

Now "The Secrets of Dumbledore," directed by David Yates from a script by Ms. Rowling and Steve Kloves, takes the stale cake for ineptitude. Eddie Redmayne, still bright-eyed and earnest as the magizoologist Newt Scamander, gets lost in a welter of minor characters of no consequence, not-so-magical beasts and successive infestations of clattering digital beetles. Whole formations of people in uniform stand around—just stand around, as if waiting for their marching orders. We're supposed to be witnessing an epic battle between good and evil, but it's a contest between energy and entropy, and entropy carries the dreary day.

## Student Rewrite:

Fantastic Beasts: The Secrets of Dumbledore Revie: Perfectly Pristine
By Mark P. Bonner

The success of the film is anticipated and ✔ well-deserved. With production at the top of its game by Hollywood's standards, every element blends together ✔ from scenery, actors, actresses, CGI, and more. While the film industry has its fill of poor movies, "The Secrets of Dumbledore," is a magical breath ✔ of fresh air.

The idea ✔ enthralls: return to J.K.. Rowling's anthology, full of creativity ✔ and the stories the world knows and loves, and travels in time to the era that shaped the Harry Potter universe ✔ before his time. Working flawlessly ✔ in 2016 when the blockbuster idea dropped as "Fantastic Beasts and Where to Find Them," Hollywood did it all over again, arguably **[yes]**even better, in "The Crimes of Grindelwald." Now we stand at the tail end of the trilogy with "The Secrets of Dumbledore," putting on an awe-inspiring performance that leaves us breathless ✔ and wondering if we could be lucky enough to see a fourth. ✔

It is a pleasure to view "Fantastic Beasts: The Secrets of Dumbledore," directed by David Yates. With a script written by the one and only ✔ J.K.. Rowling, accompanied by Steve Kloves, one will see this film exhibit an extension of a beautiful series ✔ along with the madness ✔ and fun **[GOOD]** always found in a Potter universe flick.

## The Rhetoric of Impeachment

In the middle of December, the House of Representatives passed two articles of Impeachment against President Donald J. Trump.

The Agenda and Spin Model applies to this phenomenon, of course, but it applies particularly well herein.

As reported by NBC News, the Democrats, almost unanimously, argue that impeachment is clearly imperative:

"In a lengthy opening statement, Barry Berke, counsel for Judiciary Committee Democrats, said the evidence established by the House Intelligence Committee 'is overwhelming that the president abused his power by pressuring Ukraine and its new president to investigate a political opponent' when he requested in a July phone call that Ukrainian President Volodymyr Zelenskiy launch investigations into Burisma—the Ukrainian gas company that Hunter Biden joined as a board member in 2014—and debunked conspiracies that Ukraine interfered in the 2016 election. 'The evidence is overwhelming that the president abused his power by ramping up that pressure, by conditioning a wanted White House meeting and a needed military aid that had been approved in order to get that president to investigate a political rival,' he said, adding that it was also 'clear and overwhelming that in abusing that power, the president betrayed the national interest by putting his own political prospects over the security of our country.'"

For the Republicans, who have near-unanimity as well, impeachment is a deceptive trick to stop President Trump from winning an election from a party which despises him personally but cannot beat him:

"The purpose of this hearing as we understand it is to discuss whether President Donald J. Trump's conduct fits the definition of a high crime and misdemeanor. It does not," [Steve Castor, counsel for House Republicans] said. 'Such that the committee should consider articles of impeachment to remove the president from office and it should not. This case in many respects comes down to eight lines in a call transcript,' Castor continued, referring to the transcript of the July call between Trump and Zelenskiy. 'Let me say clearly and unequivocally that the answer to that question is 'No,' Castor added, referring back to whether Trump's actions constituted high crimes and misdemeanors.

'The record in the Democrats' impeachment inquiry does not show that President Trump abused the power of his office or obstructed Congress,' he said. 'To impeach a president who 63 million people voted for over eight lines in a call transcript is baloney.

Castor went on to say that Democrats 'seek to impeach President Trump not because they have evidence of high crimes or misdemeanors but because they disagree with his policies.' This impeachment inquiry is not the organic outgrowth of serious misconduct. Democrats have been searching for a set of facts on which to impeach President Trump since his inauguration, he added.

The Democrats and Republicans disagree as to whether impeachment should even be on the House agenda. They profoundly disagree over what the impeachment focus reveals about the President and the two parties.

> It is, as all debates are, all about the struggle for agenda and spin.
> Both sides argue it is not a close call.

As you know, dear reader, impeachment succeeded but the Senate acquitted President Trump. As a rhetorical matter, impeachment and acquittal may have energized both the pro-Trump and Never Trump principals and voters for the 2020 presidential election.

As often occurs, the battle for spin in this matter reveals that both sides claim—but we have no idea whom to believe—victory in the outcomes. Both sides evidence incredulity at the other's foolhardiness and lack of ethics.

# Chapter IV

# PERSUASION AND PSYCHIATRY

CERTAINLY ONE OF THE best applications of the agenda/spin model of persuasion is psychiatry. For over 40 years I have been writing on this theoretical analysis and for most of those years in concert with my friend and then-mentor, the internationally recognized iconoclast Thomas Szasz. In fact, Dr. Szasz, author of the famous The Myth of Mental Illness, cited my theories of rhetoric in his last preface for his landmark work. This chapter explicates the rhetorical nature of diagnosing and treating nonmedical "mental illness."

## Rhetoric and Psychiatry: a Szaszian Perspective on a Political Case Study

Ever since the time of Aristotle the field of rhetoric has been loosely defined as pertaining to a rhetor's effecting of persuasion with chosen audiences. In fact, the most well-known definition of rhetoric is Aristotle's "faculty [power] of discovering in the particular case what are the available means of persuasion" (Cooper, 2000: p. 7). In this paper I shall examine the intersection between psychiatry and rhetoric and then apply that analysis to the case of 2006 Maryland Gubernatorial candidate Doug Duncan's unexpected withdrawal from that very consequential race, ostensibly due to a diagnosis of "clinical depression."

### The Production of Rhetoric

Over a generation ago, the field of rhetorical study experienced a debate over what *generated* rhetoric: was it situationally or scenically produced, or was it produced by the actions of individual persuaders or agents?

The former view was termed "the rhetorical situation" in an article by that name in the debut issue of the highly-touted journal Philosophy and Rhetoric (1968). In that article the primary cause of rhetorical discourse was cited as the situation; "Rhetorical discourse is called into existence by situation" (p.9); "So controlling is situation that we should consider it the very ground of rhetorical activity…" (p.5); and most unambiguously, "…the situation controls the rhetorical response…" (p.6).

But as this author articulated in the autonomic position to the rhetorical situation, "The Myth of the Rhetorical Situation" (1973), rhetoric is not generated by situations, it is generated by rhetors, or persuaders. In this perspective the production of rhetoric is an agent-colored, continuous competition to seek to establish the agent's own (in today's terminology) agenda and spin by making different situations

Rhetoric and Psychiatry: "A Szaszian Perspective on a Political Case Study," by Richard E. Vatz, Current Psychology, Vol 25, #3 Fall 2006 pp. 173-181. Reprinted by permission.

and facts salient and infusing them with meaning and significance to interpret the saliences for chosen audiences.

The resolution of the dispute of whether rhetoric is generated by situations or persuaders has esoteric consequences for the field of rhetoric—whether it is merely a derivative field of study or a primary one—but it also has important implications for assessing the ethical responsibility of persuaders. If rhetoric is a result of inexorable situations outside of a persuader's control, and if persuaders are significantly limited in choosing what matters to which to pay attention as well as how to give them meaning and significance, they have little or no responsibility for its depiction. If rhetoric is *not* situationally determined, then it originates in the persuader. In that case people are in control (for the most part) of that to which they create attention and the significance they give such matters. This does not deny that if the earth were hit by a continent-leveling meteor that the situation independently leads to what is the dominant issue at hand (but not the interpretations—"natural disaster?" "punishment from God?"). But short of such rare catastrophes, we live in a world of competitive rhetoric wherein saliences and meanings are persuasively fought over on a consistent basis.

There also is a tendency to follow precedent in the rhetoric of choosing and interpreting reality. This may be called *ritual*, and it refers to the similar persuasion of like situations due to their past depictions and interpretations. Thus, if past methods of creating rhetoric constitute a paradigm, it is likely through inertia that such choices in the creating of rhetoric will recur. This, for psychiatric rhetoric, if accepted ways of making salient certain behaviors and labeling them in pathological ways are extant, they will continue until the paradigm is overturned (Vatz and Weinberg, 2004). The existence of ritual, however, *does not negate the persuader's responsibility to examine the ritual of which he or she is a part.* It does explain why reliability is so often used as a false validation method of psychiatric rhetoric and practice.

Again if rhetoric is composed of persuader's choices and constrained only by the extent to which an audience will accept them, then the rhetor's responsibility for what he chooses to make salient—his or her agenda—and the meaning he or she infuses in the chosen situation—the "spin"—become that for which the persuader can be morally culpable. As this author wrote decades ago, "To view rhetoric as a creation of reality or salience rather than a reflector of reality clearly increases the rhetor's moral responsibility. We do not just have the academic exercise of determining whether the rhetor understood the 'situation' correctly. Instead, he must assume responsibility for the salience he has *created*." (1973, p. 158 emphasis in original).

The author has termed the view of rhetoric's emanating from situations the "situational point of view," and the view of rhetoric's emanating from agents who choose the agenda and its meaning or spin "the rhetorical point of view" (Vatz, 1981).

## Rhetoric and Psychiatry

Early on in my examination and critiques of the relationships between persuaders, situations and rhetoric, I argued that my articulated perspective was consistent with Thomas Szasz's implicit views on the same issues (Vatz, 1975) as well as his explicit claim that mental illness was a myth, and these positions continue to be held today (Szasz, 1961, 1978, 1987 and elsewhere). I quoted Dr. Szasz's argument (Vatz, 1975) to support the rhetorical point of view articulated in Philosophy and Rhetoric (1973): "The struggle for definition is veritably the struggle for life itself...In ordinary life, the struggle is not for guns but for [symbols]: whoever (successfully) defines the situation is the victor; his adversary, the victim. For example, in the family, husband and wife, mother and child do not get along; who defines whom as troublesome or mentally sick?...In short, he who (successfully) seizes the word imposes reality on the other" (p. 68).

(The rhetorical function of defining terms—to limit and confine debate within the interests of the definer—is a frequent point of contention against institutional psychiatry with Szasz. His work Fatal

Freedom includes a particularly cogent rhetorical analysis of the rhetoric of "defining suicide as a problem" and the constriction of debate that such a definition mandates (1999, pp. 20-22).)

Szasz was arguing that there was no way to prove that the beliefs which constituted "mental illness" existed; or that those beliefs, even if they did exist, as well as untoward or unusual behaviors, constituted something real called "mental illness." Moreover, Szasz has argued, consistent with "the rhetorical point of view," that "mental illness" cannot exist because "mental" is a metaphor, and like all metaphors is different form reality. In the two-word term "mental illness," the addition of the word "mental" to illness allows doctors to claim that there is no need to establish physical corroboration or verification.

Psychiatric rhetoric employs a number of rhetorical strategies to obviate the obligation of providing actual pathological evidence of its list of mental illnesses. First, the phrase used in the <u>Diagnostic and Statistical Manual</u> of the American Psychiatric Association (DSM-IV and soon DSM-V) is "mental *disorder*," not "mental illness" or "mental disease" (1994). The explanation of the use of this obfuscating term in the DSM-IV concedes the imprecision of the term "mental disorder:" "…it must be admitted that no definition adequately specifies precise boundaries for the concept of 'mental disorder.' The concept of mental disorder, like many other concepts in medicine and science, lacks a consistent operational definition that covers all situations" (p. xxi). Suffice it to say that there is no way to prove that any of the disorders in the DSM-IV is a disease. "Brain disease" is, on the other hand, an indisputably real entity which is physically ascertainable and demonstrable. What, then, should one make of the claim that mental illness is in reality brain disease, an argument commonly made respecting schizophrenia? Szasz has written of schizophrenia as "the sacred symbol of psychiatry" (1976). Psychiatrists choose schizophrenia as rhetorical synecdoche for all mental illness, since there may well be some who are diagnosed as having schizophrenia who actually suffer from brain disease.

Rhetorically, all uses of examples in argument are choices as examples, and it is understandable why many of the vaguer but more frequently diagnosed disorder categories such as "adjustment disorders" are virtually never used publicly to typify mental illness.

In fact, psychiatrists' strongest argument for the medical model of psychiatry is that some sufferers of schizophrenia suffer from a brain disease. Dr. Szasz's argument, an argument which is often misunderstood or ignored, is that if a patient is suffering from a brain disease and is diagnosed as "schizophrenic," that such a disease is appropriately within the purview of neurology, an authentic medical science. To call such a disease "mental illness" is a category error.

One could argue that the honest psychiatric rhetorician's responsibility is to eschew metaphors entirely and call all mental disorders "brain diseases" if this is what psychiatric rhetoricians believe mental disorders are at root. Then the medical/science conventions could be applied to determine whether the phenomena have authenticity as a disease or not, and whether some "mental illnesses" should be labeled as "brain diseases."

## Metaphorizing Behavior

One of the issues surrounding the relationship between situations and rhetoric is whether persuaders can sustain issues that have no corresponding facticity at all. Those supporting the situational point of view generally say no, but others disagree. In his highly rhetorical Animal Farm George Orwell presents his readers with the first fictional situation-within-a-situation of animals being concerned and adapting to the threat of consistent attack from humans despite the lack of such a rhetorical situation being successfully created if the audience can be so manipulated; it is thus like all situations and rhetoric: the success of presentation is a function of the ethos, or perceived authority, of the persuader and the beliefs of the audience.

This is in essence the point of view of Thomas Szasz respecting his lifelong critique of psychiatry. Psychiatry is at root a rhetorical enterprise which makes salient the most inexhaustible and creatable expanse of human unhappinesses and dissatisfactions and frames and interprets these "problems in living" strategically in medical terminology.

If mental illness is a metaphor, and if any human behavior, as Szasz argues, can be pathologized, then previously low incidence and low salience mental disorders can be arbitrarily transformed into high incidence mental illnesses. One particularly interesting example of this is "Intermittent Explosive Disorder." This is an alleged disorder whose "prevalence" is described in the latest version of DSM-IV in its entirety as follows: "Reliable information is lacking, but Intermittent Explosive Disorder is apparently rare" (p. 611).

A new study, however, finds that "Intermittent explosive disorder is a much more common condition than previously recognized" (Kessler et al., 2006, p. 669). This was determined by rhetorical legerdemain, including not medical examinations, but "lay administered diagnostic interview[s]" (p. 670), which, of course, without the rhetorical mystification means diagnostic interviews by non-physicians. These non-medical interviews include "broad definitions" of self-reported "anger attacks" and self-diagnosed loss of "control" (p. 670).

The study is then reported and interpreted by journalistic rhetoricians and linked to "road rage, spousal abuse or other severe transgressions that are totally unjustified..." (Kotulak, p. 4A). This is rhetorical creation of the existence of a new high incidence "mental illness" or "mental disorder" sufficiently certified by rhetorical means and in turn an explanation for the rhetorical creation of "road rage."

### Rhetoric and Psychiatry: a Case Study in the Case of Maryland Gubernatorial Candidate Doug Duncan

The intersection of rhetoric and psychiatry, articulated implicitly and explicitly by Thomas Szasz in scores of books and hundreds of articles and reviews, is particularly well exemplified by the events that occurred in June 2006 in the volatile gubernatorial race in Maryland.

Doug Duncan, the Democratic Montgomery County Executive in southern Maryland, was running a primary campaign which, according to various observers, was either threatening to overtake frontrunner Mayor Martin O'Malley's campaign for the Democratic gubernatorial nomination, or was languishing behind in a near-hopeless futile run. Regardless, both men were involved in an increasingly tough and tense campaign to be the Democratic nominee to oppose Republican Governor Robert L. Ehrlich in the general election in Maryland, a state with a 2-1 Democratic registration advantage.

With no apparent warning, on June 22, 2006 Mr. Duncan stunned his followers and even his opponents by announcing that he was withdrawing from the campaign because, as the front page of The Baltimore Sun worded it, "Duncan Bows Out; Candidate's depression diagnosis reshapes race for governor" (Fritze, p. 1). The facts around the diagnosis were unclear and not fully reported by The Washington Post or The Baltimore Sun, the two major newspapers in Maryland and Washington, D. C.

On talk radio, the incredulity concerning the diagnosis manifested itself in rumors being discussed that hard-nosed politics led to Mr. Duncan's being forced out, perhaps as part of an intra-Democratic power play.

The announcement by Duncan referenced "this illness" and, according to The Washington Post, cited "Duncan's health concerns" (Mosk and Marimow, p.1).

In a letter by this author printed in the Post on June 28, 2006 (Vatz, 2006) as well as in radio commentaries and discussions on 50,000 watt WBAL Radio on June 22, 23 and 24, 2006, lay the only public questioning of the diagnosis, the seemingly precipitous decision to drop out of the race, and the effect on those who had supported Mr. Duncan as well as the general public.

The rhetorical effect of the "clinical depression" diagnosis of Mr. Duncan was to freeze conventional political analysis. Typically speaking, when major political candidates drop out of a race unexpectedly, there will be articles analyzing the little-known background of the decisions, marked by reporters' using their sources, named and anonymous, to provide understanding of the decision. And this decision would seem, absent of psychiatric mystification, to raise many questions as there were not even hints of Mr. Duncan's being depressed until the week of his announcement. As the Post stated, "In recent months, as his campaign showed signs of strain—he has trailed in the polls and fundraising—neither Duncan nor his advisers gave any hint of a personal struggle" (Mosk and Marimow, p. 1). This was echoed in report after report in virtually all the newspapers.

From neither major Washington or Baltimore newspaper, the Post nor the Sun, was there any critical analysis of the politics of Mr. Duncan's decision. Instead, there were articles and op-ed pieces, such as one by predictable and perennial supports of conventional psychiatric perspectives, Kay Redfield Jamison (Jamison, 2006), which claimed to show the devastating effect that depression could have on people in general and candidates in particular, with no caveats regarding individual control in any cases.

In a memorable, representative editorial in The Washington Post (2006) there was no criticism, no investigative wondering and no skepticism regarding whether the new Democratic challenger had acted responsibly. In fact, there was no speculation whatever regarding possible ulterior motives of Mr. Duncan anywhere in print media, save the foregoing exceptions.

The editorial lavishly praised Mr. Duncan: "His disclosure yesterday suggested that in addition to his undisputed competence, Mr. Duncan possesses a streak of uncommon courage" (p. A24). What was the evidence of his courage? Because other politicians "divulged their experiences with mental illness only when forced to do so by unpleasant circumstances or news accounts; by contrast, Mr. Duncan appears simply to have told the truth about his own struggle," It did not seem to occur to the Post editorial writers in this false dilemma that they themselves had created the very "unpleasant circumstances and news accounts" that they claimed to be absent in this case, *even though they reference such accounts in the selfsame editorial*: "He was recently the subject of unflattering news stories in the Post suggesting that decisions he made some years ago may have been influenced by donations to his political account—including some arranged by disgraced former lobbyist Jack Abramoff" (p. A24).

In one final paean to Mr. Duncan and the unquestioning assumptions of the commonplaces of institutional psychiatry, the editorial says that "By discussing his depression forthrightly, Mr. Duncan may encourage others to come forward and seek help, too. Meanwhile, his many admirers will be hoping that he feels better soon" (p. A24).

Thus did The Washington Post, mystified by the rhetorical conventions of "mental illness," ignore its journalistic duties to investigate the sudden withdrawal of the Montgomery County Executive from the gubernatorial race.

The editorial did recount some of the incongruities of Mr. Duncan's withdrawal: "He decided to withdraw from the race just 48 hours after seeing a psychiatrist for the first time and receiving the diagnosis of clinical depression." Even if the Post had accepted the medicalization of Mr. Duncan's difficulties, and perhaps *especially* if the Post had accepted Mr. Duncan's explanation of this being a *medical* decision, why wouldn't they investigate the precipitousness of his withdrawal? In other words, why did not they or any other print journalistic source ask why Mr. Duncan did not seek a second opinion? Only in Thomas Szasz's "therapeutic state," wherein the pseudo-medical rhetoric of psychiatry dominates perceptions, could a politician benefit from the medicalization of his problem and yet so mystify his audience that no one asks about the requirements of a person to address seriously the issues raised if he actually *has* a disease. Perhaps this is due to the fact that on some level few really believed that Mr. Duncan has or had an illness, only that he was very unhappy. Moreover, the only two op-ed pieces pursuant to Mr. Duncan's withdrawal further militate against any hard-nosed questioning (Jamison, 2006; Moe, 2006).

Not only were no questions asked regarding Mr. Duncan's questionable handling of his disease, no questions were asked regarding even the serious political consequences of his withdrawal. In Republican eyes, even if Mr. Duncan did not win the gubernatorial nomination, he was going to be a major credible source of criticism of Mayor Martin O'Malley, Mr. Duncan's relentless attacks on 2 seminal areas of Mr. O'Malley's leadership—his anti-crime policies and his education policies—were more believable due to the *reluctant criticism* coming from a Democratic source. Reluctant testimony, or testimony by a source with values perceived as similar to the subject of criticism, is considered the most potent of persuasive rhetoric strategies. The fact that Mr. Duncan *immediately* threw his support to Mr. O'Malley was at the very least an incongruous fact, given the unrelenting nature of his criticism as well as mocking campaign ads against Mayor O'Malley (and Governor Ehrlich as well).

As far as the writer can tell, no reporter asked Mr. Duncan about the immediate nature of his cave-in. Indeed, there were other salient points about which to inquire.

Some of the other journalistic oversights, political ramifications and unintended, but anticipatable, consequences are summed up in the previously-cited letter this author published in the Post (2006) after Mr. Duncan's withdrawal:

"…[Mr. Duncan's] withdrawal is a devastating message to young people who will be on the lookout for depression as they try to navigate the travails of life. It is also further positive reinforcement for a highly suggestible public's already skyrocketing use of anti-depressants, and its increasing dependence on psychiatric help."

"His withdrawal will have profoundly negative effects on those who committed themselves to his campaign. Can and will they blame Mr. Duncan? No, he is 'sick.' Mr. Duncan indisputably was depressed during his candidacy for the Democratic gubernatorial nomination. Life indeed can be difficult. But when a high-profile politician and his psychiatric enablers give their imprimatur to the excuse of depression for bailing out, it has terrible ripple effects on our youth and other easily persuaded citizens" (p. 24).

As far as I can determine, there were no other expressions of doubt, skepticism or criticism in The Washington Post or The Baltimore Sun in the weeks following the Duncan surprise withdrawal.

## "The Rhetoric of Mental Illness and Stigma."
*by Richard E. Vatz*

Stigma Can Be A Good Thing "The Baltimore Sun (April 9, 2014)"

During an interview on the recent Fort Hood shootings committed by Army Spec. Ivan Lopez, who killed three people and then himself, CNN's Chris Cuomo suggested that Post Traumatic Stress Disorder be referred to as just Post Traumatic Stress—leaving off "disorder" because of the "stigma" associated with the term.

This is a clear example of the futility of eliminating stigma through rhetorical fiat.

It simply cannot be done. The issues is decades old, and there is little, if any, reason to believe that there will ever be the elimination or even diminishment therein of stigma, defined as a source of infamy or grace.

Mental health professionals and others wish to remove the stigma from mental illness because it will motivate sufferers to seek help and reduce the threat that a tiny percentage of them pose to others.

Last month, The Baltimore Sun reported that Maryland has funded a $1.2 million initiative, called the Center for Excellence on Early Intervention for Serious Mental Illness, for the purpose of getting "troubled people" help. ("UMBC study targets stigma of mental illness," March 22).

Their case in point is Darion Aguilar, who shot and killed two employees in The Mall in Columbia and who reportedly told a physician he was hearing voices. The physician recommended that Aguilar seek mental health counseling, but Aguilar never followed through.

There is no evidence that fear of stigma was preventing him from seeking help. Nor is there much to suggest that societal changes could influence Aguilar or someone like him to talk with a mental health professional.

In fact, there is no evidence that mental health professionals and counseling can reduce violence or even identify dangerous people better than laypersons.

Mental illness is a term which has been applied liberally to people with all kinds of problems. The Diagnostic and Statistical Manual of Mental Disorders, 5th edition, as with all of the diagnostic handbooks preceding it, includes disorders of such general nature that anyone can be so diagnosed in order to maximize "parity" with physical illness in insurance coverage. As a result, the National Institute of Mental Health estimates of mental disorder incidence now exceeds 50 percent, leading Paul McHugh, the former chief of psychiatry at the Johns Hopkins University School of Medicine, to observe incredulously "Are you kidding me?" In 2009, the American Psychiatric Association's major journal, Archives of General Psychiatry, published the estimate that "Almost half of college-aged individuals had a psychiatric disorder in the past year." These estimates cannot be proved or disproved, but they are accepted as indisputably true by most observers.

The manual does not mention the words "mental illness," preferring "mental disorder," but in public language the former term is used prolifically. It is these terms that largely account for the stigma, and no change that perpetuates the notion of diseased thinking will likely remove the shame, undeserved or not, from those so labeled.

No one who suffers a brain disease should be stigmatized, but many of the conditions labeled as "mental illnesses" involve behavior chosen through free will for which should be held responsible. Substance-related and addictive disorders, for example—including habitual use of alcohol, marijuana and hallucinogens—and self-destructive behaviors, such as gambling, are arguably a product of freely-willed decisions. Psychiatrist Sally Satel wrote less than a decade ago, in a piece titled "In Praise of Stigma" in the work "Addiction Treatment: Science and Policy for the Twenty-First Century" (The Johns Hopkins University Press, 2007) that the issue is "whether addicts' behavior can be influenced by its consequences (i.e., is voluntary). The answer is that it can." She believes that addictive behavior should be stigmatized, but not the seeking of help or the treatment process.

The answer as to whether mental illness can be destigmatized is probably "no," and part of that is due to the medicalization of behavior through the terminology of "mental illness."

The answer as to whether mental illness should be stigmatized is probably: "yes, in some cases; no in others." When mental problems are caused neurologically, brain disease should be viewed as all other diseases, but wherein problems are caused by individual choice, as in drug usage, people should be stigmatized to discourage their behavior.

*Is prolonged grief really a mental illness? penalty The Baltimore Sun,* **April 15, 2022)**

The American Psychiatric Association recently <u>added</u> another official psychiatric disorder, Prolonged Grief Disorder (PGD), to its existing hundreds of clinical diagnoses. It's described as "distinct from depression" and "marked by a pervasive yearning for the deceased."

In essence, the APA has discerned how long and how much you may be upset if you lose a loved one—say, a child—before you're considered mentally disordered.

The APA, after about a decade of internal debate, ostensibly decided to codify this new disorder so people suffering extended grief can seek treatment, however unproved the value of such treatment and the downside of such labels to the "patients."

To us, however, it appears the APA manufactures psychiatric disorders willy-nilly to nurture its self-appointed job to be nanny to the world.

In the early 2000s, amid a movement to raise the estimates of those thought to be suffering from mental illness, responsible psychiatrists like Paul R. McHugh, former psychiatrist-in-chief at Johns Hopkins University, greeted the changes with derision: "Fifty percent of Americans mentally impaired—are you kidding me?" he reportedly said. "The problem is that the diagnostic manual we are using in psychiatry is like a field guide, and it just keeps expanding and expanding…pretty soon we'll have a syndrome for short, fat Irish guys with a Boston accent, and I'll be mentally ill."

His skepticism stemmed from not just the softness of psychiatric diagnosis, but the questionable non-medical motives of those pushing new diagnoses.

In writing about the new Prolonged Grief Disorder, Ellen Barry of *The New York Times* summed it up thusly: "Its inclusion in the Diagnostic and Statistical Manual of Mental Disorders means that clinicians can now bill insurance companies for treating people for the condition…[in addition] it will most likely open a stream of funding for research into treatments—naltrexone, a drug used to help treat addiction, is currently in clinical trials as a form of grief therapy—and set off a competition for approval of medicines by the Food and Drug Administration."

Besides its lack of validity, the new disorder has the potential of adding to the psychological miseries of the "patient." To be in the midst of grieving for a loved one, now he or she must worry about whether he or she is mentally ill, i.e., grieving too long or too intensely for a decedent.

In these fractious times dependency is the major psychological problem we have to fear, and that is fostered by our viewing ourselves as always in danger of being psychiatrically disordered.

At the very least we should stop fretting that we are grieving too long for someone who has passed to satisfy pseudo-psychiatric norms as to how long we should be upset by the death of a loved one.

Jeffrey Alfred Schaler is retired professor of justice, law and society at American University, and former member of the psychology faculty at Johns Hopkins University.

*Richard E. Vatz is psychology editor of USA Today Magazine and political rhetoric professor at Towson University.*

*They are co-editors of Thomas S. Szasz: the Man and His Ideas (Transaction and Routledge, London, 2017).*

---

*Buffalo shooting makes a clear case for the death penalty The Baltimore Sun* (May 17, 2022)"

Richard E. Vatz

Jeffrey A. Schaler

On Friday, 21 people were shot in three separate incidents in Milwaukee after a Bucks' playoff game. On Saturday, police say a hate-filled teen-age racist massacred 10 citizens in Buffalo, New York. On Sunday, six people were injured and one killed in a mass shooting at a church in Laguna Woods, California.

These outrages call unmistakably for the death penalty, particularly for the perpetrator of the New York shootings. The suspect's intention, outlined in a lengthy manifesto posted online, was clear. The act, which police say he livestreamed, is also clear. Given these facts, there is no reasonable doubt about whether this 18-year-old man is guilty. He did it; he must pay for his acts. But, most important of all, the public must be protected from him and his kind.

Surely, this is an example of evil personified. The trigger may have been his nauseating racism, but he enjoyed killing.

Police say the suspect fired indiscriminately in a supermarket, injuring 13 people, killing 10 of them. According to one eye-witness account cited in news reports, the shooter "was laughing while he was being arrested." Clearly, there is no remorse, no contrition. And, of course, there were the requisite friends who said they could never imagine that such a "normal guy" could do such a thing.

That and related sentiments are irrelevant. It doesn't matter why he did it.

What then must we do?

Many criminal justice experts often assert that the classic purposes of punishment include deterrence, rehabilitation, incapacitation and retribution, yet some who are averse to capital punishment reference only—or predominantly—rehabilitation. The bottom line is that the public must be protected from these monsters. The public needs to see that the most awful, inexplicably terrorizing capital crimes will lead to the elimination of the perpetrators. That is the least we can do for their victims and future victims.

Yet, in many states, such as New York and Maryland, the death penalty has been abolished.

Perhaps some genius wordsmith can articulate for some gullible audience why the current murderous rampage should not warrant the death penalty. The usual objection is reasonable doubt. There is no doubt in the current case that this person did it.

And spare us the arguments of mental health experts—too many of whom are consistently eager to label (and testify for) anyone who was sent to get psychiatric help as "mentally ill" and therefore either cognitively not able to understand the nature of what he or she has done or volitionally unable to control his or her behavior. Clearly, those are both deceptions, what the late scholar Lon Fuller referred to as "legal fiction." The scientific and statistical truth is that we cannot know who will harm self and others with an accuracy beyond that expected by chance. If they did it before, they can do it again. There should be no second chances.

Some yearn, as they surely will in the Buffalo case, for the mental illness excuse to eliminate criminal responsibility in all possible cases. Has the perpetrator seen mental health professionals; has he been labelled as "mentally ill;" has he got a psychiatrist who says he was delusional? No matter. All perpetrators have human agency. Why did he do it? Because he wanted to kill.

The suspected shooter has been charged with first degree murder to which he has pleaded "not guilty."

The legal elements necessary to establish guilt and responsibility are well estblished, however: mens rea (the intention to commit the crime) and actus reus (the criminal act). The premeditation of this atrocity also is well-established. The gunman loaded up to protect himself and record his actions for the ages by live-streaming his massacre and wearing body armor to render useless the brave security guard who fired a shot in self-defense. That and similar behavior constitute criminal intent.

Society must stand up and show its complete contempt and rejection for the Buffalo mass murderer. We must protect ourselves from these killers clearly lacking a conscience, not pathologically, but socially. He should be, but won't be, executed. Shame on New York, which does not have the option of putting him to death but which will house him for decades. This man has forfeited his right to live by intentionally and premeditatedly mowing down over a dozen citizens.

*Richard E. Vatz (rvatz@Towson.edu) is psychology editor of USA Today Magazine and political persuasion professor at Towson University. Jeffrey Alfred Schaler (ijas@icloud.com) Is a retired professor of Justice, Law and Society at American University's School of Public Affairs, and a retired member of the psychology faculty at Johns Hopkins University. They are co-editors of "Thomas S. Szasz: the Man and His Ideas" (Transaction and Routledge, London, 2017) and authors of many pieces on psychiatry and the law.*

*Is prolonged grief really a mental illness? "The Baltimore Sun, April 15, 2022"*
Jeffrey A. Schaler
Richard E. Vatz

The American Psychiatric Association recently <u>added</u> another official psychiatric disorder, Prolonged Grief Disorder (PGD), to its existing hundreds of clinical diagnoses. It's described as "distinct from depression" and "marked by a pervasive yearning for the deceased."

In essence, the APA has discerned how long and how much you may be upset if you lose a loved one—say, a child—before you're considered mentally disordered.

The APA, after about a decade of internal debate, ostensibly decided to codify this new disorder so people suffering extended grief can seek treatment, however unproved the value of such treatment and the downside of such labels to the "patients."

To us, however, it appears the APA manufactures psychiatric disorders willy-nilly to nurture its self-appointed job to be nanny to the world.

In the early 2000s, amid a movement to raise the estimates of those thought to be suffering from mental illness, responsible psychiatrists like Paul R. McHugh, former psychiatrist-in-chief at Johns Hopkins University, greeted the changes with derision: "Fifty percent of Americans mentally impaired—are you kidding me?" He reportedly said. "The problem is that the diagnostic manual we are using in psychiatry is like a field guide, and it just keeps expanding and expanding...pretty soon we'll have a syndrome for short, fat Irish guys with a Boston accent, and I'll be mentally ill."

His skepticism stemmed from not just the softness of psychiatric diagnosis, but the questionable non-medical motives of those pushing new diagnoses.

In writing about the new Prolonged Grief Disorder, Ellen Barry of *The New York Times* summed it up thusly: "Its inclusion in the Diagnostic and Statistical Manual of Mental Disorders means that clinicians can now bill insurance companies for treating people for the condition...[in addition] it will most likely open a stream of funding for research into treatments—naltrexone, a drug used to help treat addiction, is currently in clinical trials as a form of grief therapy—and set off a competition for approval of medicines by the Food and Drug Administration."

Besides its lack of validity, the new disorder has the potential of adding to the psychological miseries of the "patient." To be in the midst of grieving for a loved one, now he or she must worry about whether he or she is mentally ill, i.e., grieving too long or too intensely for a decedent.

In these fractious times dependency is the major psychological problem we have to fear, and that is fostered by our viewing ourselves as always in danger of being psychiatrically disordered.

At the very least we should stop fretting that we are grieving too long for someone who has passed to satisfy pseudo-psychiatric norms as to how long we should be upset by the death of a loved one.

Jeffrey Alfred Schaler is retired professor of justice, law and society at <u>American University</u>, and former member of the psychology faculty at <u>Johns Hopkins University</u>.

*Richard E. Vatz is psychology editor of USA Today Magazine and political rhetoric professor at Towson University.*

*They are co-editors of Thomas S. Szasz: the Man and His Ideas (Transaction and Routledge, London, 2017).*

## Conclusion

The study of rhetoric and the assumption that rhetors generate the grounding for persuasion have been at the root of Thomas Szasz's psychiatric critiques for almost 2 generations. Only when psychiatric mystification is challenged and questioned directly can there by any unmasking of the behaviors caused by the alleged victimization claimed by psychiatric clients and their psychiatric enablers.

The case study of Democratic candidate Doug Duncan's untelegraphed withdrawal from the Maryland gubernatorial race is an object lesson on how psychiatric mystification can lead to journalists', politicians' and the general public's unquestioning acceptance of irresponsible behavior. When the rhetoric of mental illness is employed to justify otherwise unacceptable behavior, it requires rhetorical demystification to promote hardheaded examinations of otherwise unaccountable behavior and to produce demands for personal responsibility for agents' choices.

The awful stigma attached to those who are labeled as mentally ill is unavoidable, but uninformed as well. Psychiatrist and honorary persuasion expert and friend Sally Satel has it right that no one should be stigmatized for even incorrectly seeking help, but for both those labeled with mental disease categories and just the interacting with the mental health community, stigma will be unavoidable for the foreseeable future.

# REFERENCES

Bitzer, L. F. (1968). The rhetorical situation. *Philosophy and Rhetoric, 1,* 1-14.

Cooper, L. (1932). *The Rhetoric of Aristotle.* New York: Appleton-Century-Crofts. <u>*Diagnostic and Statistical Manual of Mental Disorders*</u> (DSM-IV). 4th ed. (1994) Washington, D.C.: American Psychiatric Association.

"Exit Mr. Duncan: Clinical depression sidelines a promising career." (2006, June 23) p. A24.

Fritze, J. (2006, June 23). Duncan bows out: Candidate's depresion diagnosis reshapes race for governor. *The Baltimore Sun,* pp. 1, 15.

Jamison, K. R. (2006, June 25). Acknowledging depression: Public figures perform a service in revealing mental illness. *The Washington Post,* p. B7.

Kessler, R., Coccaro., E.F., Fava, M., Jeager, S. (2006). The prevalence and correlates of DSM-IV intermittent explosive disorder in the National Comorbidity Survey replication. *Archives of General Psychiatry,* 63, 669-678.

Moe, R. (2006, July 9). What my son couldn't tell us: Mental illness and suicide must not be taboo topics. *The Washington Post,* p. B07.

Mosk, M. and Marimow, A.E. (2006, June 23). Duncan drops bid for governor: Exit pits Ehrlich against O'Malley in new Md. Terrain. *The Washington Post,* p. 1.

Orwell, G. (1945). *Animal Farm.* Orlando: Harcourt.

Szasz, T. S. (1961). *The Myth of Mental Illness: Foundations of a theory of personal conduct.* New York: Anchor.

Szasz, T. S. (1978). *The Myth of Psychotherapy: mental healing as religion, rhetoric and repression.* New York: Anchor.

Szasz, T. S. (1987) *Insanity:, the idea and its consequences.* New York: Wiley.

Szasz, T. S. (1999). <u>Fatal Freedom: The ethics and politics of suicide</u> (Westport: Praeger, 1999).

Vatz, R. E. (1973). The myth of the rhetorical situation. *Philosophy and Rhetoric,* 6, 154-161.

Vatz, R. E. (1975). Letter to the editor. Philosophy and Rhetoric, 8, 68.

Vatz, R. E. (1981). "The Forum: Vatz on Patton and Bitzer" *Quarterly Journal of Speech,* 67, 95-99.

Vatz, R. E. (2006, June 28). Dealing with depression. *The Washington Post,* p. A24.

Vatz, R. E. and Weinberg, L. S. (1994). The rhetorical paradigm in psychiatric history: Thomas Szasz and the myth of mental illness. In M. S. Micale & R. Porter (Eds.) *Discovering the History of Psychiatry* (pp. 311-330), New York: Oxford University Press.

# Brain disease vs. mental illness (Jan. 17, 2011)
*When more than 50 percent of the population is deemed sick, that validity of such diagnoses is called into question.*

> disease: n. The brain is an organ—like the bones, liver, kidney, and so on—and of course can be diseased. That's the domain of neurology. Since a mind is not a bodily organ, it cannot be diseased, except in a metaphorical sense—in the sense in which we also say that a joke is sick or the economy is sick.[1]

I have been teaching and writing for decades on the topic of "rhetoric and mental illness," arguing that "mental illness" has been a catch-all term of behavioral explanation that elucidates nothing and is often false; there is usually no "disease' in mental illness.

I have friends who are psychiatrists and neurologists who have argued with me that there is a neurological cause to some behaviors, and if that cause were called "brain disease" and proved, it would be an accurate accounting of why some violence is perpetrated.

Unlike some of my fellow critics of psychiatry, I am not an absolutist. I am convinced that Jared Lee Loughner, the accused shooter in the Tucson attack, may have had a genuine brain disease; he may be a genuinely medically ill schizophrenic. His progression of predictable symptoms seems to emanate from the classic "physical, cellular defect or lesion in a bodily organ" necessary for inferring disease.

The problem is that in discussions of "mental illness," most mental health professionals feel no constraint in helter-skelter diagnosing of mental disorders.

Not all psychiatrists are comfortable with this outlandish methodology and/or the resultant inflating of the incidence of "mental illness." A few years ago, when the National Institute of Mental Health (NIMH) estimated that more than 55 percent of the American population was suffering from some mental illness over a lifetime, Dr. Paul McHugh, the well-respected former chief of Psychiatry at the Johns Hopkins School of Medicine, incredulously and famously stated, "Fifty percent of Americans mentally impaired— are you kidding me?"

Some mental health professionals who are contemptuous of the claims of hyper-increased incidence of mental illness try to differentiate between those "mental illnesses" which are and are not "severe." But even these skeptics do not publicly argue that only a small percentage of even the "severely mentally ill" suffer from demonstrable brain disease.

First published in The Baltimore Sun. Reprinted with permission from Richard Vatz and The Baltimore Sun.

---

[1]   Interview with Thomas Szasz https://www.psychotherapy.net/interview/thomas-szasz

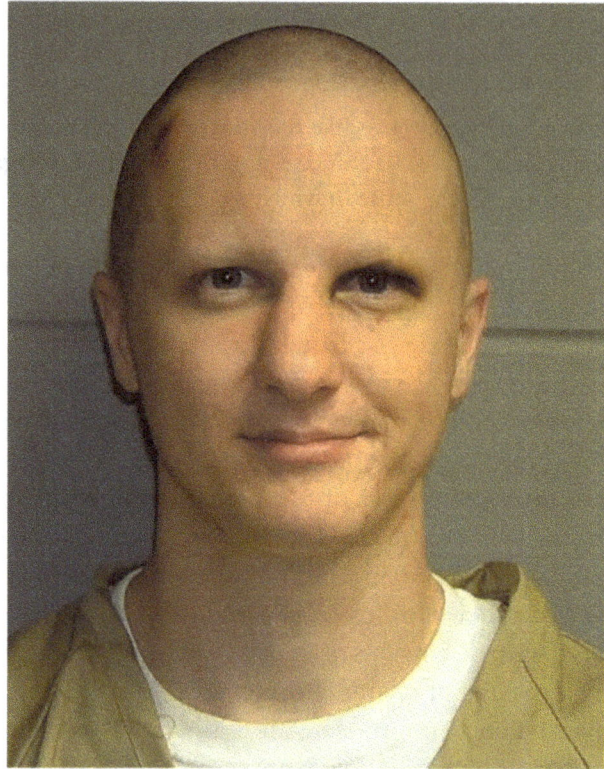

Jared Lee Loughner, a man with possible brain disease, but not meaningless "mental illness"

© Pima County Sheriff's

Congresswoman Gabrielle Giffords (D-Ariz.), a genuine victim in the Tucson shooting along with others who were shot and killed

© James Berglie/Zuma Press/ Corbis

The brutal fact is, no one knows with precision what causes most antisocial and criminal behavior: free will (perpetrator's decision; increased responsibility), disease (less responsibility), drugs (never an exculpating factor), etc. Nonetheless, indisputably, there are a few selected cases wherein no self-serving motive seems to exist, and there may be brain disease roiling the perceptions of the perpetrator.

A brain disease such as schizophrenia that can be a necessary and sufficient criterion for some violent actions should be a focus of those trying to prevent violent behavior. That well may have been the cause of Mr. Loughner's violence. But some mental health professionals, while knowing that schizophrenia accounts for only a very small number of mental problems, will falsely diagnose larger numbers of patients with it.

If we are successfully to identify the tiny percentage of people with violence producing schizophrenia, we must label it honestly as "brain disease" and end the myth of the mental illness pandemic.

"Stigma can be a good thing" by R. Vatz. First published in *The Baltimore Sun*, April 9, 2014.

# Chapter V

# EXEMPLARS OF THE AGENDA/SPIN MODEL

❖

THERE IS SOME HESITANCY to provide what I would say are exemplars of persuasion, using the agenda/spin model. This hesitancy comes from the fact that this model is practically inclusive of all persuasion, and providing "exemplars" may imply that the applications to persuasion are limited, which is not the case.

To review the primary basics of the agenda/spin model: rhetoric is (1) the struggle by persuaders to determine the subject or subjects of conversation and/or attention for chosen audiences and the relevant evidence therein and (2) the attempt to infuse the subject with the source's interpretation and/or spin.

As argued in previous chapters, all topics and subtopics of focus are determined by competing persuaders, with the exception of some matters which directly confront the empirical reality of people. If a person is shot in the chest, there is little a persuader can do to change the topic, and while there is some opportunity to struggle for interpretation ("You will be all right," "you need to see a doctor," "your friends are safe" etc.), the potential for reframing, redefining, and/or controlling the point-at-issue is in such cases limited. Similarly, but on a larger scale, if a person or a people is the target of a bomb, there are significant restrictions on available persuasion or competition regarding the struggle for saliency and/or agenda; but even in these cases of events impinging inescapably and severely on the subjective reality, there will be opportunities for competition in interpretation and/or spin of their meaning and significance.

Rhetoric by this definition is everywhere. When a child sits down for dinner with his or her parent(s), the subject of the dinner conversation is a rhetorical choice. Its meaning is, of course, as well. When Mom says, "Billie, you haven't eaten your asparagus," Billie could say, "Well, Mom, that is not a particularly interesting topic; let's talk about Dad's inability to hold a job."

But Billie doesn't have the ethos or credibility to determine either what the conversation is about or what it means.

Is Mona Lisa's smile intriguing? Why pay attention to her smile? I say, "What an uninteresting facial expression."

A point made often in this volume is that examples of rhetoric as the struggle to establish agenda/spin are everywhere. Still, there are not many that are more starkly informative than the arguments made by Supreme Court Justices Sonia Sotomayor and Samuel A. Alito on the 2011 case respecting the judicial review of whether California "had to reduce its population by tens of thousands of inmates" (Robert Barnes, "Alito and Sotomayor personify ideological split on criminal justice issue," *The Washington Post*, June 20, 2011, p. A15). The article quotes the two justices as making the following persuasive appeals:

**Sotomayor:** When are you going to avoid needless deaths that were reported in this record? When are you going to avoid or get around people sitting in their feces for days in a dazed state?

**Alito:** The majority is gambling with the safety of the people of California.

Rhetoricians would just say that the two justices are "talking past each other," but this is really a prime example of two justices struggling to persuade Supreme Court observers and others that the decision is obviously simply a question of either stopping the "torturing" of imprisoned people or (2) protecting the population from violent criminals.

Thus, it is a rhetorical contest between these two Supreme Court Justice persuaders to focus deliberation and final disposition of the case on either the consequences of crowding on prisoners or the danger to a future disposition of the case on either the consequences or crowding on prisoners or the danger to future victims of released prisoners—but not both.

Some examples of persuasion have not been recognized as such until there was dispute. Journalistic portrayal of our world was certainly not realized as rhetoric in most of the 20th century. Today, when people yearn for the "good old days" in that century, someone will point out that those days may have been good for some but they weren't so good, for example, for religious or racial minority groups. When there were fewer television networks and more conservative newspapers, the set table of issues was rarely much disputed, but with polarized media, say CNN/MSNBC and Fox, there were few today who do not realize that virtually every issue on some medium's agenda is fodder for criticism and varying interpretations. It is impossible to pick up any week's edition of *The Washington Post's* "Free for All" section, for example, without realizing that most items on that newspaper's agenda and their interpretations are up for dispute.

For much of the rest of this chapter, we shall look at illustrations of the agenda/spin model of persuasion, with the warning to the reader that persuasion in this analysis is all inclusive: that to which people are persuaded to pay attention; the meaning, interpretation, and spin that persuaders attempt to infuse into the issue made salient existing in all persuasion; and virtually all communication being a form of persuasion.

So, whereas the following list is not and cannot be exhaustive, it is meant to imply the near-ubiquity (I only say "near" because whereas I can think of no exceptions, some reader somewhere surely will, and this author does not wish that to be the salient focus of conversation of the model) of persuasion as manifested by persuaders' struggle for salience and meaning, of creation of agenda and spin.

1. President Barack Obama and Agenda. In President Obama's first term in office, there was virtually an inexhaustible number of topics that he could pursue as being his "agenda." It would have been possible to have put on the top of his list the economy, budget deficits, foreign policy (Afghanistan, Iran, Iraq, North Korea), or an array of other matters. He chose—as previously alluded to—health care. Because that was the most pressing problem facing America? No, because he could because he wanted to, whatever his motivation.

   In an October 21, 2010, *Wall Street Journal* article, Karl Rove argued, "While the economy is the No. 1 issue, the president constantly changes the subject." In every poll, Mr. Rove argues, "[T]he economy and jobs are the No. 1 issue… [y]et Mr. Obama of late has talked about immigration reform and weighed in (unprompted) on the Ground Zero mosque." In the lame duck session following the 2010 elections President Obama took a self-described "shellacking" (the Democrats kept the Senate; what would it have been if they had lost the Senate, a "catastrophe"? Could it have been a "correction?"). Through the persuasion of columnist Charles Krauthammer and others, this session was widely accepted as indicating the president was, comparable to Bill Clinton in the 1990s, "The Comeback Kid" (title of Krauthammer article in <u>The Washington Post</u>, December 17, 2010).

   The president's victories in the tax cut deal, which included a questionably motivated stimulus package, the repeal of "Don't Ask, Don't Tell," and ratification of the START treaty with Russia, opposed by Senator Lindsay Graham and others, have convinced reluctant testifier Krauthammer and apparently the political cognoscenti that Obama has effected a political rebirth, as per the beginning of 2011 ("Obama's New START," <u>The Washington Post</u>, December 4, 2010).

   Arguably, these accomplishments may not have rhetorical legs (as of 2014 perhaps, such "legs" were wobbling, it says here) or may even affect slightly President Obama's prospects for re-election, when competing rhetoricians will make salient possible failures in Mideast peace negotiations, the failure to stop Iran's nuclear program, failure in Iraq, debt crises and the issue that is not generally initiated by presidential rhetoric, the unemployment rate—near 8.2 percent as of this writing.

Reprinted by permission of Karl Rove.

"It's time to move on." This expression, pervasive when persuaders do not wish to discuss a matter that redounds to their detriment, can be interpreted as simply saying, "I wish to remove that topic from the agenda." The liberal political organization moveon. org was apparently named because that was their reaction to those who wished to discuss the issue of Monica Lewinsky with respect to the Bill Clinton presidency. What is the relevancy of that affair to the evaluation of President Clinton? There is no answer to that; it is merely a question of persuasion. Some persuaders will bring it up to this day; others will say, "You're living in the past." The effects of persuasion depend on the ethos of the persuader and the ability to raise the issue and successfully claim it is significant in the overall view of the Clinton Administration. On similar lines, in 2011 the Israel Chamber Orchestra for the first time performed music by Richard Wagner, the uniquely evil Adolph Hitler's chosen composer. Spin? Daniel Barenboim, the renowned Israeli pianist and conductor, actually said, "It is time to 'move on.'" Chamber Orchestra Chief Executive Eran Hershkovitz said, "It is the best response and proof that they [Nazis] did not succeed and will not succeed;" Elan Steinberg, deputy head of the American Gathering of Holocaust Survivors and their Descendants, characterized the decision to play Wagner as a "disgraceful abandonment of solidarity with those who suffered unspeakable horrors by the purveyors of Wagner's banner."

2. There has been a flurry of outrages concerning air traffic controllers who have fallen asleep on the job and thus endangered incoming flights which had to land "blindly." Many people infer that this has not happened before, but, of course, it is simply the case that the issue was not previously brought to a national audience, and there was no meaning or spin ascribed to the matter(s). As NBC News reported on April 15, 2020, the fact, not the issue of air controllers' sleeping on the job from time to time has been around for years.

3. International terrorism became an issue in this country on September 11, 2001, years after Osama bin Laden declared war on the United States. Is it a criminal matter or is it a matter of international catastrophic significance? At an earlier point Attorney General Eric Holder was content to allow "terrorists" to be defined and therefore interpreted as "criminals" who should be tried in civilian courts. The correct depiction and significance depends not on "reality," but on which persuader is successful in providing the interpretation or spin. President Obama seems to find it more significant now that he supervised or appeared to supervise the killing of Osama bin Laden. What is the meaning of his killing? Well, according to the president, it is "the most significant achievement to date in our nation's effort to defeat al Qaeda," and it was pursuant to his, president's, making bin Laden's killings or capture "the top priority of our way against al Qaeda." (http://www.npr.org/blogs/thetwo-way/2001/05/02/135908803/video-and-text-of-the-presidents-statement-on-death-of-bin-laden) Is his execution evidence that, as the president said in his speech announcing bin Laden's demise, "America can do whatever we set our mind to," or is it evidence that in many way "Osama bin Laden is the victor?" (http://www.cbc.ca/news/world/story/2011/05/02/neil-macdonald-osama-bin-laden.html?ref=rss&sms-_ss=facebook&at_xt=4dbec8c03710e638%2C0) The interpretation is a struggle—always.

4. There are few better ways to understand the agenda/spin model than through the example of the Sarah Palin phenomenon. In 2008 senatorial candidate Senator John McCain single-handedly made a little-known and virtually unvetted "in-your-face" choice for his presidential running mate, Alaska's Governor Palin, perhaps to show his detractors that he would rather be cantankerous than be president. In today's parlance, she went viral and has been the object of nationwide attention and discussion, agenda and spin creation until the Trump Administration. It can be persuasively

argued that she gave Senator McCain a fighting chance in a losing cause or that she scuttled any chance he had to win. Incidentally, this writer has made the latter persuasive case. I must point out parenthetically that one of the worst proclivities of both Democratic and Republican U.S. presidents has been to choose vice presidents dangerously unqualified to be president: Henry Wallace by Franklin Delano Roosevelt, Dan Qualye by George H. W. Bush, and John Edwards by John Kerry, just to name a few. This is just another area wherein Ronald Reagan's responsible example should educate future presidents, Presidents who are adjudged "great," but who, if they had died in office, would have been replaced by utterly unprepared or irresponsible vice presidents, illustrate yet another example of the inexhaustibility of facts to make a persuasive argument. If F.D.R. had been replaced by pro-Communist Wallace and if there had been a negotiation to end World War II, the outcome might have led even Rooseveltophiles to revile President Roosevelt. It might be said as well, however, consistent with the arguments of this book, that Roosevelt supporters might have found other facts and interpretations to marshal in support of his memory regardless. Note, of course, that many Democrats had no problem ignoring the success of the "surge" of the Iraq War in President George W. Bush's final days as president, and that many Republicans had a problem in quickly crediting President Obama with his successful "get" of Osama bin Laden.

In the 2012 presidential election Mitt Romney did not allow his Vice-Presidential choice to be made into a bellwether issue. Polls have historically indicated that never, including 2008 with Alaskan Gov. Sarah Palin as nominee, has that choice been material in the public's vote for president. But for those not mystified by public opinion polls, the effect of the virtually unvetted, polarizing Palin may have swung the election. Not all persuasion manifests itself in public opinion polls. Romney's choice for Vice Presidential nominee was not easily made into a presidential issue.

Fort Hood Assassin Major Nidal Hasan: Mentally ill or crazy like a fox?

© HO/Reuters/Corbis

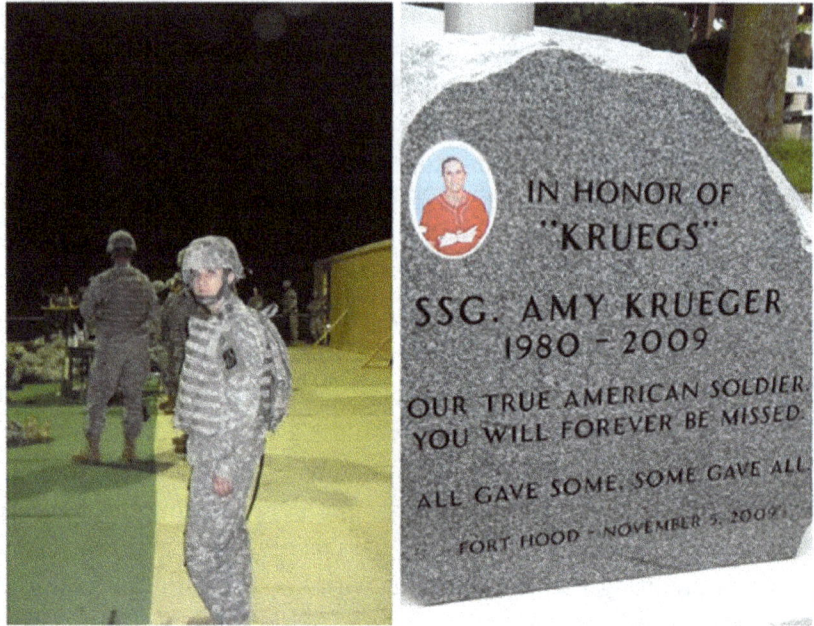

A high school principal said about murder victim Sgt. Amy Krueger, "I just remember that Amy was a very good kid, who like most kids in a small town are just looking for what their next step in life was going to be and she chose the military…she…really connected with that kind of lifestyle and was really proud to serve her country."

© Christopher Morris/VII/Corbis

5. The persuasive competition in foreign policy is a never-abating phenomenon, but recently there may be no better example that the contest over what allegedly threatening country or issue deserves salience in public discussion of foreign policy. The Obama Administration talks about and takes military action against Libya, belatedly discusses Egypt and takes no such action, virtually ignores the anti-government riots in Syria, and from 2009-2011 ignores the dangerously nuclear-acquisitive Iran. When the president orders the Navy Seals to capture or kill Osama bin Laden, he (President Obama) and most of the media for a lengthy period of time disregard all of these problems, save the possible effect of bin Laden's killing on the terroristic threat of al Qaeda. It is not, of course, my goal to assess the sagacity of these rhetorical choices—although I do not lack such opinions—but merely to point out the power of controlling the issues to be highlighted: what is made salient or part of the national agenda and what meaning/spin competing national actors wish to put on these issues.

6. One tremendously interesting example of the strategy of leaving out information for purposes of creating persuasion, however, is in the case of the public discussions of Major Nidal Hassan, the terrorist who effected the Fort Hood massacre, but was interpreted widely by non-Administration sources as being motivated by psychiatric problems.

   There has never been any dispute regarding his perpetrating the killings, although in legal settings there may be rules requiring a presumption of innocence in the proceedings.

   What is more fascinating is the rhetoric from military sources, rhetoric in which, as summarized by Dorothy Rabinowitz of *The Wall Street Journal*, "Every branch of the military issued a final report on the Fort Hood massacre. Not a single one mentioned radical Islam."

   As summarized by Ms. Rabinowitz and uncontradicted by any other source,

   In this report, titled "A Ticking Time Bomb" and put out by the Senate Committee on Homeland Security and Governmental Affairs, there is a detail as dazzling in its bleak way as all the glowing misrepresentations of Dr. Hasan's skills and character, which his superiors poured into their evaluations of him. It concerns the Department of Defense's official report on the Fort Hood killings-a study whose recital of fact made no mention of Hasan's well documented jihadist sympathies. Subsequent DOD memoranda portray the bloodbath-which began with Hasan shouting "Allahu Akbar!"—as a kind of undefined extremism, something on the order, perhaps, of work-place violence.

It continues:

This avoidance of specifics was apparently contagious-or, more precisely, policy. In November 2010, each branch of the military issued a final report on the Fort Hood shooting. Not one mentioned the perpetrator's ties to radical Islam. Even today, "A Ticking Time Bomb," co-authored by Sen. Joe Lieberman (I., Conn.) and Susan Collins (R., Maine), reminds us that DOD still hasn't specifically named the threat represented by the Fort Hood attack-a signal to the entire Defense bureaucracy that the subject is taboo.

Rabinowitz cites the fact that to fulfill Walter Reed's requirements in his becoming a psychiatrist that Hasan was required to make a presentation on a psychiatric theme and that "Hasan proffered a draft consisting almost entirely of wisdom from the Quran arguing for the painful punishment and liquidation of non-Muslims."

In the interpretive phase of rhetoric surrounding Major Hasan, the military characterized his motivations as due to "mental illness," not Major Hasan's Islamist sympathies and detestation of the West.

Since persuasion is often an ongoing phenomenon, it should not be surprising that pursuant to counter-persuaders' opposition to this initial interpretive rhetoric, the government would oppose an exculpatory psychiatric disposition of the case and charge Hasan in a court-martial, with death as a possible outcome, while leaving still the possibility that Hasan could himself claim to be motivated by insanity. The quickness of the media, on the other hand, to label the Norway mass murderer a "conservative" serves as quite a rhetorical contrast (http://www.humanevents.com/article.php?id=45145).

7. As indicated earlier, trials are all about persuasion: what is admissible as evidence, salient, what is the credibility of the participants, of the issues and matters the judge and jury are to adjudicate, etc. In 2011, the verdict in the Casey Anthony case, wherein a 25 year-old's daughter (2-year-old Caylee) died, has been rendered, with the jury's finding the accused not guilty of first-degree murder, aggravated manslaughter, and aggravated child abuse.

Here is some of what we ask as scholars of persuasion:

1. Why was this case given such salience by so many media throughout the country?

2. What evidence was focused on and what was ignored? Why?

3. What is the believability of Casey's parents? Should the defense's accusations of sexual assault against Casey's father have been considered at all? Alternatively, should Casey's mother's claim of computer search for "chlorophyll" and "chloroform," the latter of which the prosecution claims was used to kill her daughter, be relevant?

4. In the jury's interpreting the evidence for the verdict, what is the meaning of "beyond reasonable doubt?" Does it not vary from criminal jury to jury? From case to case?

The student of persuasion is not necessarily in a better position to render a just disposition on legal cases, including this one, but he or she is in a position to account for how persuasion worked.

At the risk of oversimplifying, if the jury had not been persuaded that defendant Anthony's life was in jeopardy from the death penalty being imposed, it is this persuasion professor's opinion that the verdict would have been guilty, as least for aggravated manslaughter and aggravated child abuse. The prospect of the death penalty for an attractive 25-year-old, non-threatening defendant, foolishly made salient by the prosecution, was a major factor in effecting the verdict. If, in addition, the jury had been convinced that "beyond a reasonable doubt" was not tantamount to finding circumstantial evidence insufficient, a guilty verdict on the major incarceratable offenses would have been quite more likely. Prosecution persuasion needed some correctives, perhaps by those knowledgeable of the Agenda/Spin model.

8. All of the writing of history is revelatory of persuasion, of course, as it involves creation of agenda/spin. In an article by Robert McCartney in *The Washington Post* ("Textbook needs to lose its liberal tone," July 7, 2011, pB 1) he writes reluctantly (McCartney is a self-confessed progressive, or [more pejoratively] now a "liberal") about a controversy originally made salient by Fox News and then-correspondent Glenn Beck wherein a third-grade social studies book in Frederick County, Maryland, in McCartney's words was "unmistakably slanted to the left in numerous places." The book, still according to progressive McCartney, "pushes pro-environmental views," tax-supported

child-care, profiling only liberals as examples of "individuals who have made a positive difference in their communities," and more. All books of social studies and history and other social sciences choose what to include and not include (agenda) and choose the interpretations therein (spin). When you hear the question, "what will historians say about 'x'?", the answer should always be some variation of President Richard Nixon's (do you see many positive citings of Nixon in academic texts?) answer to Henry Kissinger's observation that history would treat the president more kindly than his contemporaries: "That depends on who writes the history."

A perfectly informative answer by a man who understood authentic uses of persuasion, despite his own inability at the end of his presidency to be persuasive.

9. All political campaigns are persuasion campaigns: struggles over what to talk about, what to ignore (salience/agenda), and what highlighted events mean or do not mean (spin). Take a look at the nine-and-a-half minute grilling by Chris Wallace on Fox News in April of 2012 regarding the President Obama agenda-creation of the alleged debt and deficit-salutary "Buffett Rule" by which taxes would be raised on wealthier Americans. Wallace questions Buffett regarding the surprising math of the "Millionaires' Tax" proposal, which yields $47 billion in contrast to the $6.4 trillion added to the deficit in the next ten years. Everything one needs to understand about persuasive changing of the subject or topic and infusing different meanings can be seen in this exchange. Ask yourself if you have ever seen a more nervous respondent as well. This video is exquisitely valuable for understanding persuasion. http://www.youtube.com/watch?v= BhkcpiwembE

10. One of the traditional debating issues in America is capital punishment. This is a persuader's dream issue because there is no end to citing that which is included and excluded in the debate. In addition the spin is also limitless: how do you infer whether the death penalty is a deterrent when its use is so variable and deterrence is so unprovable? Again, recognizing that all sides can make a persuasive argument for or against this final exit punishment, here is a piece I wrote regarding persuasion in the state of Maryland on this matter (per a February 23, 2013 Maryland "Red Maryland" blog). Please read it to analyze the topic, persuasion in one locality on the issue, and the author's use of rhetoric:

## Saturday, February 23, 2013
### Capital Punishment: Questions for Death Penalty Repeal Supporters
—*Richard E. Vatz*

In 2007, New Jersey became the first state to abolish the death penalty legislatively. Saved from execution, among others, was Jesse Timmendequas, who, according to CNN, "lur[ed] Megan Kanka into his Hamilton Township home to see a puppy, then rap[ed] her and strangl[ed] her."

As a professor of persuasion for over 40 years, I have been struck by more than the illogic of those legislators seeking repeal of the death penalty. According to Patch.com, Sen. Bobby Zirkin argues that his change of heart on the issue is based on the utterly selective and unrepresentative "testimony of some victims who said the death penalty provided little closure because of lengthy appeals" and the irrelevant observation of the fact that "the state hasn't executed anyone in nearly a decade."

But I have been more disturbed by the lack of repeal supporters' publicly engaging the critical arguments at all.

Please allow me to ask the following important questions to legislators and others, questions which should be addressed-or should have been addressed-before the state of Maryland repeals capital punishment. Failing that, these are questions for which voters in a referendum should seek the answers before sustaining the end of executions.

1. If there is a Newtown in Maryland with children massacred, will you stand by your vote for the repeal of the death penalty?

2. If a convicted first-degree murderer orders killings from prison, how would you stop this? What should be the punishment if one or more murders are carried out? Why would a murderer necessarily ever stop if there is no death penalty?

3. If a convicted first-degree murderer kills inmates or prison guards, what should be the punishment?

4. If you base your vote on public opinion polls, does your position vary if that measured opinion changes? After Timothy McVeigh murdered 168 people in the Oklahoma City bombing, a USA TODAY /CNN/Gallup poll indicated that 81% of the public felt he should be executed.

5. If you argue that capital punishment is racially biased, would you agree that the major source of that conclusion, the Paternoster study, argues that the race of the defendant does not produce a disproportionate use of the death penalty, only the race of the victim does so. Do you not agree that this could be changed and is largely an effect of the disparities in geographical use of the death penalty?

6. If you argue that capital punishment is not a deterrent, are you moved by the fact that *The New York Times*, hardly a bastion of capital punishment support, reported in 2007 that according to about a dozen studies "executions save lives. For each inmate put to death, the studies say, 3 to 18 murders are prevented"? A study by Emory University echoes this position and argues that decreasing the time between conviction and execution would also save lives. This may be because executions delayed create the perception of no executions.

The lack of implementation and the lengthy time of disposition of executions should not be the basis for eliminating them. It should energize Maryland to shorten the period between conviction and execution.

The fear of a mistake can be alleviated by raising the standard of proof, if need be, to "beyond any doubt." That would also eliminate the possibility of serial murderers continuing their grisly behavior.

Even a death penalty unused, but utilized for plea bargaining, is superior to not having its availability.

Regardless, to act in such a definitive way to save murderers from executions deserves a full addressing of the issues, not a rush to irresponsible action.

11. Political Interviewing, more now in the hyper-contentious age of political rhetoric than ever, is often an overt rhetorical enterprise with the interviewer's competing with the interviewee for agenda and meaning. One of the very best interviewers of the times is Fox News Channel's Tucker Carlson, founder and former editor of *The Daily Caller* [full disclosure, I have published in *The Daily Caller*].

Nightly with nary an exception, Carlson battles one or more of his interviewees for agenda and spin. Typically, he will say to his subject, "but you have ignored the question" and some variation of "I'm going to come back to the original question until you answer it." Sometimes he will openly laugh quasi-pleasantly when the person being interviewed answers a question with a complete non sequitur.

Agenda and Spin: what shall we talk about and what does it mean?

The following is an exchange between Carlson and Philip Levine, the Mayor of Miami Beach, on June 1, 2017, on the topic of Donald Trump's pulling out of the Paris Agreement on global warming. The exchange quoted was chosen for its prototypicality of Carlson's interviews.

**Carlson**: I'm just wondering how this specific agreement, sending three million dollars a year to countries like India and China who don't have to lower their emissions rates, is going to fix the global warming problem in Miami Beach.

**Levine**: Tucker, let me tell you what is going on in Miami Beach. When I became Mayor, we had streets that were flooding. During sunny days the water levels have gone up dramatically. We, of course, moved forward to raise our roads, put in pumps, change our building codes, and it's not because we are so excited to have to do this, but we have to do this for the survival of not just Miami Beach: its coastal cities all over the world.

**Carlson**: Okay.

**Levine**: Tucker, I heard what you had to say, but I have to tell you something: when the world's leading scientists are telling you this is what is going on, I mean, and some of the smartest minds in the world are saying this is the reason why, at some point you have to listen.

**Carlson**: You are actually dodging my question completely. I am not denying the existence of sea level rise, I am merely asking a very specific policy question. If this is about policy, how will the terms of agreement, handing three million dollars per year to China and India who do not have to lower their emissions in the rest of this generation, how will that help what's going on in Miami Beach as you just described?

**Levine**: Tucker, the bottom line is the world is getting too hot and the oceans are rising, and that is affecting Miami Beach and is affecting all coastal cities. We must cool the globe down.

**Carlson**: I can't let you, I can't let you dodge it again, okay. Because at the end, the specifics, the specifics make the difference.

**Levine**: I'm not dodging.

**Carlson**: It is dodging. I am asking about a very specific agreement that you and everyone else is beating their chest about and Trump "destroying;" okay, fine; I am open-minded; okay, tell me how that specific agreement and the financial arrangement in it will help the problems we just described.

**Levine**: I am going to tell you why, first of all, I am not the guy from the left what I can tell you is this: I am in the radical center; I call myself a radical centrist.

**Carlson**: You're dodging again.

**Levine**: The bottom line is rising oceans are not Republican and they are not Democrat. What will an agreement do? The agreement puts the world together in one alignment and says we have a problem; let's work together and solve the problem. I mean, Tucker, knowing there is a slight chance—what if there is a slight chance, Tucker, that all the world's scientists and some of these great minds—let's just say they are right, and, if they are, maybe it's a good idea and we can do something about it.

**Carlson**: What you are saying—hold on—what you are saying [is] I don't have to bother to learn any of the details about a very specific agreement that we are all mad about today because there are people's names who I don't know who think it's a good idea. My question to you is why wouldn't the average person say "Hey I am open-minded but why don't you tell me more; give me some specifics; don't force me to participate. Explain to me; it's a democracy, after all, right, isn't it?"

12. In discredited Sen. Al Franken's book, humorously but not humorously titled "Al Franken: Giant of the Senate," his political persuasion per the struggle for agenda and spin is clearly evident. As National Public Radio describes it at their website, Franken says the strangest skill to learn was the art of the 'pivot'—essentially, ignoring reporters' questions. 'If someone said, 'Why are you 20 points behind?' I explained, 'Well, you know, we have a long time to go.'

His campaign staff quickly shut that down. 'They'd say, 'No, no, no—just pivot! Just say, 'Minnesotans don't care about the polls. What they care about is their kids' education and whether they're going to go bankrupt if they get sick.' 'It took me forever to learn how to do that,' Franken says."[1]

*The Washington Post* adds, "If a reporter asked him about trailing in the polls, for instance, he practiced with his spokespeople how to dodge: 'My instinct would be to answer the question. But that's not what you're supposed to do. You're supposed to say, 'When I go around the state, Minnesotans don't talk about the polls. They talk about their kids' education…' And so on… Franken finally learned his lesson after an unhelpful *New York Magazine* story, and he still marvels that in-state journalists let him get away with it: "A couple of days later I had a sit-down interview with a Minnesota print reporter who had interviewed me a number of times before. I have no recollection of the actual content of the interview, but I distinctly remember the thrill of using a new skill. Right out of the box, I pivoted to avoid answering a perfectly valid question so I could instead talk about whatever it was I was supposed to talk about that day. And the reporter seemed just fine with it! So I did it again on the second question. Again, the reporter seemed to have absolutely no problem. On the next question, just for the hell of it, I really overdid it, pivoting gratuitously. Again, I completely got away with it.'"[2]

13. The Fallacy of the Whataboutism Fallacy
Richard E. Vatz, Ph.D. May, 2021

In the endless rhetorical armory for non-substantively disputing arguments, we have now in the public lexicon during the Trump years the fallacious concept of the informal fallacy of "whataboutisms." Loosely defined, whataboutism is theoretically trying to change the agenda invalidly in an argument from one subject to another. It is typically used by progressives to direct conservatives' agenda.

The problem is, who is to say which subject is valid.

Informal logical fallacies are more than ways to identify illogical or unreasonable arguments, as sometimes the "fallacies" are linked to reasonable, almost indisputable claims. George Floyd's killing was met with people's concern about the widespread violence that accompanied some of the protests. Liberals shouted, what else: Whataboutism!, even when many of those pointing out the destructive and deadly violence sincerely conceded the appalling killing of Floyd.

---

[1]    Scott Detrow, "Sen. Al Franken Embraces 'The Funny' Again in New Book," NPR http://www/npr. org/2017/05/30/530262824/sen-al-franken-embraces-the-funny-again-in-new-book May 30, 2017

[2]    James Hohman, "The Daily 202: How Al Franken learned to stop being funny and love the Senate." July 3 https://www.washingtonpost.com/news/powerpost/paloma/daily-202/2017/07/03/daily-202-how-al-franken-learned-to-stop-being-funny-and-love-the-senate/59598742e9b69b7071abca2e/?utm_term=a6cd57341c82&w-pisrc=nldaily202&wpmm=1

The informal logical fallacies, such as ad hominem, straw man (now straw person of course), faulty analogy arguments etc., are themselves inherently debatable and could be labeled with one of the other informal fallacies, "name calling." The fallacy du jour, whataboutism, is a particularly appropriate new strategy for today's cancel culture, seeking to eliminate relevant counterarguments. Derived from the similar but Latinate, and therefore less available for proliferate discrediting to everyone, fallacy of tu quoquo (you also), whataboutism claims are paradoxical: they mean, let's ignore your argument and focus on my argument, which you claim is not relevant.

I am famous (or infamous) in my field of Political Rhetoric for my Agenda-Spin theory of persuasion, a theory I first propounded almost one half-century ago and reiterated in my recent book, *The Only Authentic Book of Persuasion: the Agenda-Spin Method*. Oversimplified, the theory argues that all of persuasion is a struggle for what we talk about and what it means. It is applicable to almost all political disputes, but it also references persuasion in fields as disparate as psychology/psychiatry and everyday conversation.

The charge of "whataboutism" is, again, to say that a person is fallaciously trying to change the subject of a conversation or dispute. It is the struggle for agenda and spin, the elements of all persuasion.

So if an anti-Trump source, say CNN, wants to talk about the president's alleged collusion with the Russians to sabotage American elections, and a pro-Trump source says, "That is a false issue; the issue is Vice President Joe Biden's trying to help his son Hunter by threatening to retract one billion dollars in loan guarantees for Ukraine unless a prosecutor was fired," the initial source, or both, can accuse the other of using a whataboutism. Generally, in a presidential election, if the economy is going well via stock markets, but there is a wide gap between the haves and have-nots, the two sides will emphasize their issue by accusing the other of engaging in whataboutism. Classically in law, the cliche of the law implying whataboutism has its presence in the Carl Sandburg lesson: "If the facts are against you, argue the law; if the law is against you, argue the facts."

Perhaps the top professor in the history of rhetorical studies (Dr. Trevor Melia of the University of Pittsburgh) used to say "logical fallacies are rhetorical strategies." Implicitly, he was saying that several ways to disparage others' arguments ostensibly through identifying logical fallacies were simply methods to support the spin of their own arguments.

Another fallacious fallacy accusation rampant in today's political lexicon is "virtue signaling." The purpose of this sometimes true and sometimes false but never provable accusation is that there is bad motivation from an advocate of a position through his or her argument. It is a worthless, non-substantive distracting argument. The answer to the irrelevancies of "whataboutisms" and other informal logical fallacy accusations is to argue only facts, albeit all fact are selected facts, and devote time to all sides' major arguments. If your opponent's arguments are inconsistent and/ or irrelevant, state why they are such.

Otherwise, your arguments are nothing but "name-calling," which, parenthetically, is what "name-calling" is as well.

14. To close my exemplars of the Agenda/Spin model of persuasion, let me provide a choice of quotes from one of the few consensual heroes of American history, about whom it is not just frequently but nearly always said some variation on, "He is one of the great, if not the greatest, American Presidents. He emancipated the slaves and gave his life to do so. He was a saint:"

   "I have no purpose, directly or indirectly, to interfere with the institution of slavery in the States where it exists. I believe I have no lawful right to do so, and I have no inclination to do so."

Yes, that is from the First Inaugural Address of Abraham Lincoln, given on March 4, 1861. When Lincoln is discussed, when movies are made about him and when the issue of presidential dispositions on slavery is discussed, one rarely if ever hears this quote. President Lincoln was likely trying to avoid war as long as possible and used persuasion to that end.

Why?

Because it is a choice piece of evidence (pun intended) that complicates most persuaders' message: that Abraham Lincoln was always an unalloyed opponent of slavery and waged a war to end it.

Finally, one of the best examples for understanding agenda and spin competition is to look at the House Select Committee hearings on the January 2001 Capitol attack. The hearings were broadcast on every major network, save Fox, which implied their centrality of importance. There were no such hearings on what Fox maintained were more critical issues: inflation, exploding crime in America—including the illegal protests at their homes against conservative Supreme Court justices and their anticipated decision eviscerating a 1973 Supreme Court decision, Roe v. Wade—the capture of a would-be assassin of Supreme Court Justice Brett Kavanaugh, the energy crisis and the border crisis.

Within the hearings was the issue, virtually ignored by the mainstream press, of the violation of Congressional protocols by Speaker Nancy Pelosi's blocking two of House Republican leader Kevin McCarthy's choices for the committee: Reps. Jim Jordan and Jim Banks. Instead, the Speaker chose the two most virulently anti-Trump Republican Representatives, Rep. Liz Cheney and Adam Kinzinger. Regarding spin, in her long speech on the floor, quoting Trump in order to demonstrate his complicity in encouraging people to go and riot at the Capitol, Rep. Cheney intentionally cropped his statement wherein Trump stated, "Go in peace and love."

To Democrats and the left there has hardly been a more material set of hearings, analyzing a time when American democracy was teetering on the edge…To Republicans and the right, it was much ado about nothing, distracting from major issues threatening democracy in the United States.

## Unfair advantages are the rule in college admissions, not the exception
*The Baltimore Sun*, March 22, 2019

The late, brilliant comedian Joan Rivers' favorite catchphrase was "Grow up!" It was said in jest, but meant in earnest to wake her shocked audiences from their stupor long enough to realize that her comedic targets were doing horrible things all the time.

It is in this same spirit that I urge the nation to "Grow up!" in its understanding of the university admissions process. The incredulity expressed upon the "discovery" that television stars Lori Loughlin, Felicity Huffman and other high-powered principals conspired to fraudulently get their children and others entrance into elite colleges and universities is itself incredible.

While the individual criminality of the particular perpetrators—both applicants and school officials—is somewhat surprising, the academy, despite its claims of devotion to Lady Justice style blindness, has never been very meritocratic in its admissions practices.

The god-term in universities today is "diversity"—a goal articulated ostensibly to rectify past discrimination committed, in part, against groups, mostly minorities, who couldn't gain fair admission to higher education in the past. But the policies only selectively redress such unfair and unequal treatment: Jewish, Catholic and other disfavored applicants for most of the history of higher education were either not admitted to major universities or were limited by a quota system, but there are few compensatory initiatives at colleges and universities intended to redress those actions.

In fact, Harvard University's infamous race-conscious admissions policy has literally gone on trial. In the words of *The Chronicle of Higher Education*, "The case, brought by a nonprofit group called Students for Fair Admissions Inc. …claims the university discriminates against Asian-American applicants by limiting the number of those students it admits."

Admission departments, often with little or no oversight within schools of higher education, arbitrarily establish priorities for small or large percentages of those they admit, including—in addition to varying weightings of grades and SAT and/or ACT scores and class rankings—such largely immeasurable factors as letters of recommendation, the reputation of your high school, your writing ability in essays, your outside interests, etc. Applying to an admissions officer who was a wrestler? You might be advantaged if you wrestle in high school.

The well-regarded College Board, on its website, states well the random array of entrance criteria in admissions policies around the country: "Geographic location, racial or ethnic background, extenuating or unusual life circumstances and experience living or studying overseas may all be influential."

Equally significant are attributes that are rarely written down: Money, societal position and legacy status are classic considerations among the non-meritorious criteria at most colleges and universities. Different colleges and universities allow admittance according to which relatives have gone there previously; in what sports applicants excel; how famous, wealthy and significant are the applicants' friends and kin; and generally whom they know.

There is no excusing the criminal fraudulent behavior in the scandalous college admissions bribery case now in focus nationwide, but let's not have crocodile tears implying that this is the only salient aspect of unfair competitive advantages in the academy: They are the rule, not the exception.

*Richard E. Vatz, professor at Towson University and member of its University Senate for over 40 years, is author of "The Only Authentic Book of Persuasion: the Agenda-Spin Model" (LAD Custom Publishing, 2019) and the co-editor of "Thomas S. Szasz: the Man and His Ideas" (Transaction Publishers, 2017). He can be reached at rvatz@towson.edu.*

# Chapter VI

# THE PERSUASION OF CANDIDATES AND PRESIDENTS DONALD J. TRUMP AND JOE BIDEN

◆◆
◆◆

*On Friday, November 18, 2016, Richard E. Vatz gave a lecture at West Chester University (Pa.) and the Rhetoric Society of America. The audience of about 100 students, including faculty and administrators, demonstrated that there are college audiences pursuant to a fractious election who wish to consider and debate, not protest, its outcome. The following has been only slightly edited:*

## "The 2016 'Agenda' Presidential Election:" When Presidential Rhetoric Went Wacky

I AM HONORED TO be chosen by West Chester University of Pennsylvania and the Rhetoric Society of America to speak to you about the presidential campaign recently completed which, depending on to whom you listen, adumbrates either the end of the world as we know it, or knew it, or the Second Coming. As one who voted for neither the odious candidate or the other odious candidate, I feel I may be in a unique position to declaim on the rhetoric of the campaign.

It is important when one is lecturing on the rhetoric of a national election that the speaker say what are his biases and what he means by rhetoric and be clear about why it is so important. My biases, well known in my university, Towson University, and my national organization, the National Communication Association (NCA), for better or worse, are conservative...not the nasty alt-right or fake conservatism, as in Breitbart's Steven Bannon, but Howard Baker, George F. Will, Paul Ryan, or Mitt Romney anti-big government, pro-individual responsibility, pro-internationalism in foreign policy conservatism. I have counted the number of similarly minded faculty at the NCA, and I counted twice to ensure I could report to you the exact number of such people there. Including me, and remember I counted twice to ensure I had an exact number, there are...uh...two or so.

But whereas most colleges and universities, outside of Michigan's great Hillsdale College, where I gave a lecture a couple of years ago (following the year George F. Will spoke, I might braggingly add), treat their conservative minority badly, my university, Towson, is one of the institutions of higher learning that actually believes in and protects academic freedom and treats its ideological minority quite well, save an ex-president and one faculty member and one staff member whose names you do not know and do not wish to know. In any case I am prepared to add West Chester University to the good list.

On to what rhetoric is.

Rhetoric, as defined by your speaker's book, *The Only Authentic Book of Persuasion: the Agenda-Spin Method*, a controversial work in my field, is the struggle for agenda, or the subjects we talk about, and the struggle for spin, or the meaning and significance of what we talk about.

In presidential campaigns the agenda and spin are always critical. In the 1960 race, with which many of you are, no doubt, familiar but will not be old enough to recall, the contest was between Vice President Richard Nixon and Massachusetts Senator John F. Kennedy.

The rhetorical conventions were all broken that year. Why would an 8-year Vice President, Nixon, debate a little-known second-term senator? The debates put the then relatively obscure Jack Kennedy on an equal state with the well-known Nixon. People could see how polished, cool and attractive Kennedy was and how sweaty and unattractive Richard Nixon was. It was a consensually validated truth, and I think it actually true nonetheless, that people who heard the debates on radio thought Nixon had won them, but people who watched them on television thought that Kennedy had won them going away. Incidentally, Nixon made an incredible rhetorical mistake serially that no one reported as such but which Americans noticed, perhaps only unconsciously. Frequently, Nixon—he was nick-named "Tricky Dick," a less devastating title than "Crooked Hillary" as it turns out—when asked to respond to a Kennedy position would sometimes say "I have no comment."

I did part of my doctoral dissertation on Nixon's rhetoric.

Let me tell you what this does-saying "no comment"—to an audience: it communicates that Nixon's opponent, Senator Kennedy has said it all on a particular point, that Nixon had nothing to add, and that there were no major differences between the two nominees. That raised people's comfortability with the upstart Kennedy, who, parenthetically, was only 4 years younger than Nixon, 43 to Nixon's 47. Everyone remembers the old Nixon versus the young Kennedy, but that was only true metaphorically.

Then Kennedy pressed as dominant issue in the campaign the matter of what the United States would do if Red China, as it was then called, would attack Quemoy and Matsu, two islands far from Taiwan, and he managed to make himself seen as a safe overseer of nuclear weapons, which he may have been, since he solved the Cuban Missile Crisis. But no one has ever mentioned Quemoy and Matsu materially again to my knowledge.

I should probably point out, however, to Kennedy worshipers, of which I was and sort of still am, that there is a strong body of opinion that we would not have even had a Cuban Missile crisis were it not for the fact that Soviet Premiere Nikita Khrushchev likely miscalculated what the United States would do if the Soviet Union put nuclear missiles-albeit under Soviet control-in Cuba…the first time such weaponry would have been in the Western Hemisphere outside of the United States. Kennedy was perceived as weak, allowing Fidel Castro to stay in power, and folding in the Bay of Pigs invasion several months after JFK took office.

Fast forward to 2016, following 2 elections in which matters of agenda control dominated the presidential election. There were many reasons why John McCain, war hero, would likely win in 2008, but to make a long story short, once he chose Sarah Palin after vetting her to the tune· of one quick conversation, he was not going to beat the historic candidacy of Barack Obama, especially since not just the media, but John McCain as well, would not bring up as part of his campaign agenda Obama's relations with radical leftist Bill Ayers, gangster Tony Rezko, who gave Obama a loan for his house in Illinois, and active America-hater Jeremiah Wright, for years erstwhile minister to Obama and author of violent rhetorical attacks against America, as in, and please excuse me, "God damn America!" and others.

In 2012 many pundits anticipated debates and national discussions over President Obama's arguably overly passive foreign policy and then-apparent failure substantially to grow the economy.

Instead, when Romney was unknowingly recorded as saying that he started with 47% of the public supporting government handouts and against him, Chuck Todd had a reportorial orgasm and almost single-handedly made that the issue of the campaign. Romney contributed to the diminishing of his campaign agenda when, after a surprisingly weak first debate by Barack Obama, Romney followed it up with a second debate in which he in effect took foreign policy off the table by announcing that his [Romney's] views and those of the president were quite compatible. To those of us who were and are Romney fans, this was stunning, but yet another example of former President Nixon's dictum that the time to be most careful is when you have won a round in a persuasive fight. Your guard goes down.

## The 2016 Election

This year has been unique in presidential campaign rhetoric, although it contains some time-tested and unfortunately well-precedented rhetorical elements. Hillary didn't want to discuss domestic issues like the $20 trillion and rising national debt. She swore she would not add a penny, despite liberal economist and co-founder of the Center for Economic and Policy Research Dean Baker's having said in an interview just before the election, "Clearly, she is going to add to the debt [the debt comprises, among other elements, Medicaid, Medicare, Social Security, national defense]." Nor did she want to discuss government spending, taxes, disincentivizing fatherless homes, or attaching with American and allied soldiers ISIS strongholds or soldiers, which several years ago were fewer than 5000 strong in Iraq and, according to military reports, eminently eradicable.

So what issues did the presidential election include and exclude in 2016?

Here is some of what the 2016 presidential election comprised, including to the detriment but full cooperation and complicity of arguably the most irresponsible Republican candidate in memory, perhaps ever:

1. Donald Trump's gratuitous attacks on John McCain as not a real hero, as Trump famously put it, [Politico] "He's not a war hero," said Trump. "He was a war hero because he was captured. I like people who weren't captured."

2. Trump's insistence until recently that President Obama was not born in the United States and claims that the falsehood began with Hillary. [When Mrs. Clinton was asked whether she believed Sen. Obama's claim regarding being born in this country, she responded, "I take him at his word."]

3. Trump's contradictory positions on abortion, his denial of ever supporting the war in Iraq despite video evidence to the contrary, and his support of United States action in Libya despite video evidence to the contrary.

4. Trump's claim that the election was "rigged," and his plan "to look at the results at the time of the election" to perhaps not accept the results if he didn't win dominated much of post-debate national discussion. He did grant that he would not question the results if he won, which he did, and he has not, for those who doubt his integrity, this would change in 2020, however.

5. Trump's crude language regarding women: "And when you're a star, they let you do it…Grab them by the p—y…you can do anything." Trump denied committing sexual violence through tastefully incredulously asking people to notice the unexceptional looks of his accusers.

Here are some issues included to the detriment of Hillary:

1. Hillary's Benghazi oversight as Secretary of State and her claim that she did not tell relatives of the deceased that the deaths were caused by rioters influenced by an anti-Muslim video, despite contemporaneous notes to the contrary. [She told parents of the victims that it was a video and the same day e-mailed her daughter to say it was terrorists.]

2. Hillary's health and her fall when she had pneumonia.

3. The argument that it was time for a woman to be elected president—rhetorically speaking, to whom does that argument appeal after the first couple of months campaigning? Does it add additional voters? Hard to see how.

But the election was mostly about Donald.
Here are some virtually-overlooked issues that were never fully discussed in the campaign:

1. The "pay for play" accusations against Hillary Clinton, issues which she simply ignored in the third presidential debate, after the matter had been mentioned in the first and second debate.

2. What would Hillary and Trump's economic policies be?

3. What would Hillary and Trump's foreign policy be?

4. Trump wants to deny protection to NATO countries that don't pay their fair share—is he serious? Since the election, Trump has not reiterated this position, but he has prodded them for payment. Several of the NATO nations now have actually paid and more fully support the organization.

5. The release of American hostages from Iran and the payment of 400 million to the Iranian Government in violation of the law preventing the government from paying ransom for hostages.

Now, the final debate included a number of substantive, important agenda matters, but, as with the second debate, in the days following, the issue was Trump's possible refusal to accept the election outcome and the rhetorical deportment of Trump at the A1 Smith Dinner in New York, typified by Trump's gracious and subtle humor:

"Here she is in public pretending not to hate Catholics." So the bottom line is we had another agenda election, with critical issues of domestic and foreign policy being excluded from the election agenda.

The final question is, "Who should have won this election?" It pains me to say that neither of the two principals deserved to win the election.

For a year leading up to the election, I met no one who was excited about Hillary's becoming president. I met no one who defended all of Trump's tasteless personal attacks. I met no one who was secure with Trump's being Commander-in Chief.

I met a lot of people who thought Donald Trump was the only option to change the direction of the country.

Richard E. Vatz teaches political rhetoric at Towson University and author of *The Only Authentic Book of Persuasion*

## Donald Trump: Unusual Candidate and Exemplary Presidential Persuader

The candidacy of Donald Trump resulted in the presidency of Donald Trump and the phenomenon of a man who has meticulously followed the Agenda-Spin model, even though there was and is no evidence he was or is aware of it.

Throughout his political climb, then mere citizen Trump complained that the press was emphasizing matters that should not have been part of agenda and employing spin that constituted "dishonesty."

The primary mark of Donald Trump's persuasive communication is that he, to understate the matter, rejects diplomatic niceties. His consistent referring to Democratic candidate Hillary Clinton, with whom he was quite friendly before he became interested in the presidency, as "Crooked Hillary" was just one example of his rejection of the niceties in the protocols of conventional presidential persuasion.

What follows are some analysis of Trumpian presidential persuasion as well as articles that I have published during the presidential campaign. I am including an article written in *The Baltimore Sun*, August 10, 2016, which contained, I would argue, spot-on analysis of the persuasive strategies of then-candidate Trump but which incorrectly included the anticipation that Trump would lose the presidential race. He fought and fights for his own agenda, and where I was mistaken was in the belief that he would fail in succeeding to make his agenda the campaign agenda. Persuasion works precisely as described in this book, but I wanted to illustrate that such analysis does not mean that all predictions per that analysis will be correct.

Also below is an article from January 18, 2017, wherein one can see the instability of President Trump's working agenda and spin, how today's focus is not tomorrow's and today's enemy is tomorrow's friend and vice-versa. The article speculates on how such unstable persuasion can lead and may lead to military and political catastrophe. Also included is an article dated October 20, 2016, which was published in MarylandReporter.com, on the final presidential debate of 2016. This article describes the best debate of the 2016 presidential campaign regarding the focus on stock issues and the slight deemphasizing of interpersonal slights.

For a representative look at President Trump's political rhetoric, here is a video of his first major news conference in the East Room of the White House, February 16, 2017: https://www. nytimes. com/2017/02/16/us/politics/donald-trump-press-conference-transcript.html?_r=0

In that press conference the president set off a firestorm, as predictably he will do for his entire presidency, with unconventional changes of agenda and spin. He focused on his alleged popularity and talked about his polls to prove it, but cited only Rasmussen Reports, the poll which typically is higher for Republicans and was the only one as of that debate which showed Trump enjoying majority support.

He focused on the media, a focus that no president has made part of his agenda since Richard Nixon: "The press has become so dishonest that if we don't talk about it, we are doing a tremendous disservice to the American people. Tremendous disservice. We have to talk about it. We have to find out what's going on because the press, honestly, is out of control. The level of dishonesty is out of control." Later in the press conference Trump stated: "I'll tell you something. I'll be honest. I sort of enjoy this back and forth, and I guess I have all my life, but never seen more dishonest media than frankly the political media. I thought the financial media was much better and more honest, but I will say that I never get phone calls from the media."

Among other characterizations of the significance of the "dishonest" press, Trump said that the dishonest media affect the agenda of the presidency: "I'm saying, here's my chief of staff [Reince Priebus], a really good guy, did a phenomenal job at RNC, I may have won the election, right, won the presidency, but we got some senators, all over the country, take a look. He's done a great job. I said to myself, you know, I said to somebody there, look at Reince working so hard putting out fires that are fake fires. They are fake. They are not true. Isn't that a shame because he'd rather be working on health care. He'd rather be working on tax reform, Jim [Jim Acosta of CNN]. I mean that. I would be your biggest fan in the world if you treated me right."

The rhetoric and persuasion of President Trump is unique among presidents in the modern presidency. He makes agenda and spin a consistent fight with the press, and he often wins that fight.

## Vatz: Trump wins final debate, but self-destructs on accepting election results From Maryland Reporter

*By Richard E Vatz October 20, 2016*

Suspense was high surrounding the final debate between Hillary Clinton and Donald Trump, as media outlet after media outlet wondered whether Trump could "turn it around" and warned "this could be Trump's last chance" (Scott Pelley on CBS Evening News, hours before the debate) in their final clash, moderated by Chris Wallace.

In the history of presidential debates since 1960, after the first debate, most elections were little changed by subsequent debates, as voter sentiment becomes solidified. That said, a debate focusing on domestic and foreign policy differences is always worthwhile and could at least shore up Donald Trump's support. The latter two thirds of the second presidential debate focused on issues to Trump's advantage. But in that debate's subsequent days, the easily distractible Republican challenger talked nothing about such issues, only how outrageous were the charges of sexual assault against him and how unattractive were his accusers. Campaign manager Kellyanne Conway criticized his slurs against the women.

So the nominees entered this debate with new issues, including Wikileaks on the Clinton campaign; Hillary's admission in speeches that she says different things to different audiences; that her aides find her two-faced and often don't believe her; as well as other embarrassing revelations, such as the Project Veritas videos which evidences Democrats plotting violence at Trump rallies.

Finally, Trump argued repeatedly that the election is rigged and that Hillary has been using illegal drugs to shore her up.

Donald Trump again brought potentially embarrassing supporters to the debate, including President Obama's half-brother, Malik; and Patricia Smith, the outraged mother of Sean Smith, who died in the attack on Benghazi. Hillary Clinton brought the Dallas Mavericks' opportunistic owner, Mark Cuban, and a woman fired by Donald Trump.

Despite distractions, it was a good debate.

### The debate

The evening started off well with moderator Wallace insisting the audience be quiet. No one has articulated why there should be an audience at all, but a quiet audience is the next best thing. There was no handshake by the candidates.

Most people wanted a substantive debate, and this one was the most substantive.

Thanks to Chris Wallace's oversight, material issue after issue was brought up, but many of those that redounded to the detriment of the candidates were ignored. But this is how you moderate a debate with the two difficult people who loathe each other.

This was Donald Trump's best performance, but he refused to concede he would accept the results. The elephant may have squashed the fact that tonight's agenda included so many major domestic and foreign concerns.

Among the major issues and their impact that were brought up and pursued or not pursued:

A. **No surprises:** Re Supreme Court nominees, Hillary said that she wanted jurists who will protect minorities and stand up for people's rights. Trump ·emphasized his support for the Second Amendment, which Hillary unconvincingly claimed she did as well.

B. **On abortion,** Hillary would protect it and Trump opposes it, but Hillary's insistence that late-term abortions should be allowed could not give her additional votes.

C. **On Immigration,** Trump accused Hillary of supporting amnesty and open borders, and she never denied it, and his accusation was sustained by Wikileaks revelations. (She said she was talking about energy.)

D. **On Trump's chumminess with Vladimir Putin,** Trump looked naive, but later he criticized Hillary effectively for being fooled by Putin's machinations in the Middle East.

E. **Missed opportunities for Trump:** Hillary stated her support for raising the minimum wage, making college debt-free per Bernie Sanders and her caving to his policies, and pre-school for all students, another added cost. Trump never addressed any of these: what the late Paul Tsongas would have called acts of a Pander Bear.

F. **The economic debate went to Trump.** He emphasized the anemic growth rate, the administration-long stagnancy and the doubling of our national debt. Wallace asked if she would follow Barack Obama's policies, and Hillary ignored the question. Point made; response avoided.

G. **Fitness.** Wallace asked about their relative fitness to be president, which led to the accusations against Trump about his treatment of women being discussed. Hillary effectively listed the incredulity-producing rhetoric of Trump, past and present, from his tasteless attack on the looks of his accusers, his attacks on John McCain, his attacks on federal judges, etc. There was no pressure by Wallace or Trump for her to defend her attacks on husband Bill's alleged victims and paramours.

H. Wallace raised the question of the serious "pay for play" allegations against the Clinton Foundation, a question that got no response from Hillary, as she once again pointed to the good things it had done. Trump asked why the Clintons took money from countries which persecuted and murdered gays. Hillary again did not address the issue. Hillary at that moment broached the issue of Trump's tax returns and why he paid no federal taxes for many years. Trump inexplicably simply responded that it was legal to do so. He should have emphasized his losses which made it possible or not addressed it at all.

I. Wallace asked Trump if he would accept the results of the election regardless of who won, and Trump said he will look at it at the time and that Hillary should not be allowed to run. This answer dominated reaction to the debate...Donald's mistake.

J. Trump discussed the indisputably foolish policy of the **United States' telegraphing its foreign policies**. Hillary ignored the issue. Trump further criticized the foreign policy of the Iran deal and American losses in the Middle East, and Hillary ignored Wallace's question of what she would do if she imposed a no-fly zone and Russia violated it—would she shoot the plane down? Hillary ignored the question.

**Overall:** Trump made material criticisms that were ignored by Hillary, and he left unanswered whether he would accept the election results if he lost. That dominates the immediate reportage—not wise. Chris Wallace was near-perfect. It is hard to stop two candidates from talking over each other completely, but he ensured a wonderful addressing of material issues.

*Professor Vatz teaches political persuasion at Towson University and is author of "The Only Authentic Book of Persuasion"*

## The Baltimore Sun
## The problem with Trump's rhetoric
*August 10, 2016 Richard Vatz*

**Op-ed: Trump highlights irrelevant personal issues in place of those that raise opposition toward Mrs. Clinton**

In rhetorical study, we know that presidential campaigns are essentially persuasion campaigns that comprise agenda—the issues discussed—and spin, essentially the way they're discussed.

In 1960, the question of what to do if "Red China"-as it was called then-imperiled the islands of Quemoy and Matsu became the focal point of a major debate and campaign dispute between John F. Kennedy and Richard M. Nixon in their close election. Kennedy made Quemoy and Matsu into a representative issue that illustrated how he and Vice President Nixon differed in their dependability in handling nuclear weapons policy. And he won the election.

That was the first agenda struggle in the modern presidential campaign era, but it would be the kind of competition that clearly is important in all elections and was decisively important in 2008 and 2012-and maybe in 2016, as well.

The failed campaigns of John McCain and Mitt Romney in 2008 and 2012 respectively can be attributed to their lack of control of agenda and spin, especially agenda, and the contrary effort by much of the media to discuss issues that are secondary. To his detriment, Mr. McCain largely ignored associations of Sen. Barack Obama that could have devastated the senator's campaign, such as his interactions with radical leftist Bill Ayers, felon Tony Rezko and the anti-Semitic, anti-American Rev. Jeremiah Wright. The media, unsurprisingly, did not focus on them either.

Unlike Mr. McCain, Gov. Mitt Romney's campaign wasn't undone by what he left unsaid, but by what he said, specifically his claim that "there are 47 percent of the people who will vote for the president no matter what." They are people, he continued, "who are dependent upon government, who believe that they are victims, who believe the government has a responsibility to care for them, who believe that they are entitled to health care, to food, to housing, to you-name-it. That that's an entitlement. And the government should give it to them. And they will vote for this president no matter what."

Chuck Todd of NBC in particular along with other major progressive media sources played "gotcha" with this statement, and turned it into a permanently salient issue in the campaign, minimizing focus on the then-struggling economy and the president's foreign policy.

In 2016, Donald Trump also faces a hostile media, but unlike Mr. Romney, he is more than complicit in the negative coverage: He helps to minimize attention paid to issues that benefit him and to maximize issues that detract from his popular and electoral support.

The consistent criticism from those who don't want Hillary Clinton to win the presidential election has been that Donald Trump won't stay on message; he highlights irrelevant, often out-of-date personal issues in place of issues that raise opposition toward Ms. Clinton. Megyn Kelly of "The Kelly File" expressed her bewilderment over this earlier in the month, asking "What is he doing relitigating every controversy from the primary season?" And in response, Benjamin Domenech, the publisher of The Federalist noted that "It is like this every day."

No significant supporter of Mr. Trump has even attempted to publicly articulate a compelling reason for the presidential candidate's attacks on the parents of the heroic Capt. Humayun Khan, who was killed in action in Operation Iraqi Freedom, sacrificing himself to a suicide bomber and likely saving the lives of hundreds of soldiers nearby. It is an American commonplace that such Gold Star parents are to be left uncriticized and particularly left uncriticized repeatedly.

Such rhetorical problems make Mr. Trump's agenda perfect for Hillary to maximize her Democratic and centrist Republican support. His campaign is doomed without a change in course, though it may already be too late for even that. An attempt to capitalize on Hillary Clinton's recent slip of the tongue, saying she "may have short-circuited" the truth regarding the FBI's investigation of her emails, became not an indictment of her trustworthiness, but a means to question her sanity-an issue that has been repeatedly raised about Mr. Trump himself.

Perhaps Mr. Trump was hoping to deflect his own mental fitness scrutiny, aware of what befell Mitt Romney's father. In the 1968 presidential contest, George Romney rhetorically self-destructed when he explained that his early opinion supporting the Vietnam War was due to American generals' having "brainwashed" him. The media jumped all over him, and his candidacy never recovered.

As has been pointed out, Ms. Clinton said she had short-circuited her answer, not that she herself "short circuited." Again, by making the issue personal rather than focusing on her deceptions, Mr. Trump avoids making her untruths an agenda issue.

If he continues to allow minor personal matters and petty grievances against Hillary and irrelevant others to become dominant issues, and to ignore the issues that will devastate his opponent, his election agenda will preclude victory.

*Richard Vatz has taught political persuasion at Towson University for four decades and is the author of The Only Authentic Book of Persuasion: the Agenda-Spin Model (Kendall Hunt, 2013). His email is rvatz@towson.edu*

For the first time in over 50 years, the country, during the administration of President Trump, is experiencing an inward look at the amount of rhetoric-related violence in the United States. At the time of this writing, June 20, 2017, there has been perhaps more political violence in the country in the last few months than at any time since the 1960's. In that period, just to name a few of the appalling events that transpired, one should cite the assassinations of President John F. Kennedy, his brother Robert F. Kennedy and Medgar Evers, the murders of civil rights workers, Andrew Goodman, Michael Schwerner and James Chaney, the final years of lynching of African-Americans and the general tenor of violence mostly throughout the south and the mood throughout the country.

In 2016-2017 there have been murderous attempts on the lives of Republican congressmen; Black Lives Matter's public chantings of "What do we want? Dead cops; When do we want it? Now;" and "Pigs in a blanket…fry 'em like bacon;" comedian Kathy Griffin's carrying around of a mock-up of a bloody severed head of President Trump; the Huffington Post's suborning Jesse Benn in an online journal's piece in 2016 in which he called for "A Violent Response To Trump;" and the Shakespeare in the Park production sporting Donald Trump-like actor as Julius Caesar, killed fictively but bloodily in a stabbing assassination.

Neither was the president blameless.

At his rallies, Mr. Trump seemed to warm to the idea of violence as a panacea for…violence, saying "So if you see someone ready to throw a tomato, knock the crap out of him, would you…seriously…I will pay for the legal fees, I promise…[and] You know what they used to do with guys like that [obnoxious protesters] when they were at a place like this [rally]…they'd be carried out on a stretcher, folks"[1] These are typical of the many irresponsible pro-violence-spins President Trump has used.

The liberal electronic and print press has covered the targeted attempted murder against the congressmen as either less important to the overall issue of violence, and/or they have sought to spin it as linked to irresponsible ·actions by conservatives. Witness *The New York Times* take before a subsequent correction: "In 2011, when Jared Lee Loughner opened fire in a supermarket parking lot, grievously wounding Representative Gabby Giffords and killing six people, including a 9-year-old girl, the link to political incitement was clear…[B]efore the shooting, Sarah Palin's political action committee circulated a map of targeted electoral districts that put Ms. Giffords and 19 other Democrats under stylized cross hairs." [2]

Yet, the conservative electronic and print press has discussed the issue of violence in America as if there has been no incendiary rhetoric from the president whatsoever.

As always, it is all about agenda and spin…what is made part of the discussion and what does it mean. It is all a function, again, of the struggle for agenda and spin. This is no more the case with President Trump than it has ever been. The only change is the intensity of the struggles.

---

1.    CNN Newsroom Transcripts http://www.cnn.com/TRANSCRIPTS/1603/12/cnr.07.html

2.    Kruzel, John, "No evidence Sarah Palin's PAC incited shooting of Rep. Gabby Giffords," PunditFact, June 15, 2017. http://www.politifact.com/punditfact/statements/2017/jun/15/new-york-times-editorial-board/no-evi-dence-sarah-palins-pac-incited-shoot-rep-/

## *The Baltimore Sun*

*January 18, 2017*

## Putin: Friend or foe?

*Richard E. Vatz*

**Op-ed: A friendship with Putin is less a problem for Mr. Trump than a rivalry would be.**
Dominating recent political news is the debate over whether Donald Trump is being played for a fool by Russian President Vladimir Putin.

The media are rife with incredulous panic that Mr. Trump is insufficiently concerned about Russia's alleged Hillary hacking, and so rigid in his support of Mr. Putin that he could become even more complicit than President Barack Obama in enabling Russia's global expansion.

A bigger concern, however, should be whether Mr. Putin is about to fall out of favor, particularly after the recent release of salacious and unverified opposition research alleging the Russian Bear would attempt to blackmail Mr. Trump.

Donald Trump's friends have a way of becoming enemies-and his enemies, friends-in a flash. Mr. Trump once said Ben Carson engaged in "total fabrications," for example, dismissing him as "sleepy" and more low energy than Jeb Bush. Then he made him a cabinet member. And Twitter is full of examples of the president turning on a dime to overreact to a new enemy or make a new friend of a previous enemy.

Earlier this month, Meryl Streep, the brilliant and largely uncontroversial actress, criticized President-elect Trump in her acceptance speech for the Cecil B. DeMille Award at the Golden Globes. She scolded him in sadness for mocking a disabled New York Times reporter during the presidential campaign.

Mr. Trump's response was predictable for candidate Trump but somewhat surprising and dismaying-and worrisome-for President-elect Trump: "Meryl Streep, one of the most over-rated actresses in Hollywood, doesn't know me but attacked last night at the Golden Globes." He denied attacking the reporter but added that Ms. Streep was a "Hillary flunky."

I voted for neither Mr. Trump nor Ms. Clinton for president, but I have consistently specified that my major worry regarding a Trump presidency was that his volatile personality in a nuclear age-including his flying off the handle pursuant to personal slights or changes of perception of various principals—could lead to unpredictable explosions, figurative and literal.

Regarding Russia, Mr. Trump has consistently claimed that "Having a good relationship with Russia is a good thing, not a bad thing. Only 'stupid' people or fools' would come to a different conclusion."

But Mr. Trump may already be heading to reassess his friendly perception of Russia, acknowledging last week that the country was the likely culprit behind election hacking.

Remember: Mr. Trump hates being perceived as a patsy—hates it.

Once president, what if Mr. Trump finds an unrepentant President Putin who continues to ignore and flout United States interests in Syria, the genocide for which Mr. Trump has excoriated Mr. Obama?

The most frightening specter is not a President Trump who is overly friendly and compliant with Mr. Putin; it is a President Trump who believes Mr. Putin has played him for a fool and who overreacts. Hell hath no fury like a President Trump scorned.

*Richard E. Vatz (rvatz@towson.edu) is professor of political communication at Towson University and author of "The Only Authentic Book of Persuasion."*

## The Ad Hoc Rhetorical Presidency of Donald J. Trump

When my daughter was 3, 4, and 5 she would, like all children that age, become agitated and cry seemingly uncontrollably at times when she was hungry, thirsty or in need of elimination or had some pain or itchiness or irritation. My wife and I discovered that at the same time my daughter was fascinated by trucks. Why? We don't know to this very day, although, in her mid 30's, she is not currently so focused on trucks. But whenever we were in our living room or on the road and she was terribly upset by some unknown source, we would say, "Look, there's a truck?", whether or not there was one. She would immediately stop crying and look for the truck and not cry again until the next time.

I am not 100% comfortable comparing the President to a toddler or a pre-schooler, as it is unfair to discerning small children, but he, like them, is prone to adhocracy, paying attention to the most recent item at which someone can grab his attention.

The President is an ad hoc issue dealer, per his Art of the Deal, abetted by the Media, particularly the anti-Trump all-the-time media comprising, among others, *CNN*, *MSNBC*, and major newspapers, such as *The Washington Post* and *The New York Times'* news and editorial op-ed pages. People who detest Trump and his rhetoric range from those who point, understandably, to his lack of outrage at the racist and the anti-Semitic marches in Charlottesville, to his allegedly weak responses to the appalling actions of President Vladimir Putin and Russia in Syria and the Ukraine, to the lack of presidential outrage at the murder of journalist Jamal Khashoggi and Saudi Arabia's complicity, to, less understandably, the beginning of trade wars with China, to his raising of the national debt through the lowering of taxes, to his warlike rhetorical exchanges with China, to his suborning an alleged threat against Stormy Daniels and others, with whom he is alleged to have had affairs.

I am reminded of the famous humorous observation by Mark Twain, repeated for many locales but, parenthetically, not Maryland, "If you don't like the weather wait a minute, it'll change."

With a small number of politicians who are ad hoc political rhetoricians, and most particularly, Donald Trump, if you don't like the issue being discussed, or if you don't like the president's position on it, wait an hour or a day or two, and it will change.

Trump is the only president in the history of presidential debates who would not accept the agenda put forth by the questioners and in his answers moved to other agenda items, for example, but not exclusively, Hillary's alleged perfidiousness and law-breaking. Throughout his presidency, he has and will talk willy-nilly about the above issues with a different agenda and spin.

What about his apparent antisemitism, per his shocking and horrible passive reaction to the Charlottesvillian marches? He is the first president who is going to build a U.S. Embassy recognizing Jerusalem as the capital of Isreal, and he announced his intention to move the U.S. Embassy from Tel Aviv. President Trump's support of the Jewish State is manifold, evidenced, for example, by Prime Minister Benjamin Netanyahu's support of him.

Trump has been accused of starting a trade war with China, but subsequent to this threat, China has telegraphed an intention to compromise, despite critics' attacks of the danger of his (Trump's) inciting a devastating trade war.

Has Trump raised the national debt irresponsibly? Perhaps, but said attacks from Democratic leadership are perhaps the most inconsistent lines of criticism by Democrats, per the Obama Administration. Of course, Republicans have a comparable awful records on this as well.

A Stormy Daniels scandal? When asked about this allegedly pressing but in reality not-so-pressing issue, Trump focuses on the fellow who threatened Daniels' child and his problematic sketch that looks like Stormy Daniels' former husband (and, to this writer, Richard Chamberlain), calling it "a total con job." No one, one can predict, will ever be identified from this picture.

Suborning the consistency adhocracy, or persuading audiences as to what are or is considered the issue or issues of the day, are the media agenda and spin, motivated by the inveterate detestation of Donald Trump by the progressive media.

I read and watch a tremendous amount of right and left—that is, moderately right and left—print and electronic media from the *Wall Street Journal* to the *Washington Post* to *Fox* to *MSNBC* to *CNN*.

One day at the height of North Korean news, I believe it was—although it might have been on the heels of the United States attack on Syria's chemical weapons—I turned to CNN for a half an hour, and all they covered was Stormy Daniels, again, that nice adult entertainment lady who accused the president of having sex with her and paying her through Micheal Cohen $130,000, which she claimed did not allow her to tell her politically important story. Also, as always, the Russian collusion story was covered and covered and covered and covered. Of course, now Ms. Daniels' lawyer has been discredited, so he is rarely covered by CNN at this time, 2019.

I have not much empirical evidence of CNN's yellow journalism used against Trump, but as *The Hill* reported in 2017, "The undercover video from conservative sting artist James O'Keefe showed a CNN producer questioning the network's coverage and suggesting important stories had been buried to keep the focus on Trump and Russia…[T]he video appeared at a difficult moment for CNN, however, which was just forced to retract a story alleging that one of Trump's associates had improper dealings with a Kremlin-backed bank. The episode led three of CNN's reporters to resign and reinforced the notion among many conservatives that the network is hell-bent on taking Trump down…"

And *The Hill* also told of one of a number of reports of the CNN bias against the Trump presidency: "A Harvard study found that CNN's coverage of Trump was negative 93 percent of the time over the course of his first 100 days in office." [The Hill 6/27/2017]

Short of an actual outbreak of war, President Trump and the mainstream media, namely Fox, MSNBC, CNN, and the major networks, appear to be engaged in arbitrary agenda creation, adhocracy and consistent spin, leaving the public nowhere to find serious agenda creation in Trump, his supporters or critics.

There is no longer a disinterested source for hungry news aficionados to find [Vatz, Richard E. August 2, 2018. Letter to the Editor. "It's impossible to find a disinterested view of this presidency." *The Washington Post*].

## The Rhetoric of Impeachment

In the middle of December, the House of Representatives passed two articles of Impeachment against President Donald J. Trump.

The Agenda and Spin Model applies to this phenomenon, of course, but it applies particularly well herein.

As reported by NBC News, the Democrats, almost unanimously, argue that impeachment is clearly imperative:

"In a lengthy opening statement, Barry Berke, counsel for Judiciary Committee Democrats, said the evidence established by the House Intelligence Committee 'is overwhelming that the president abused his power by pressuring Ukraine and its new president to investigate a political opponent' when he requested in a July phone call that Ukrainian President Volodymyr Zelenskiy launch investigations into Burisma—the Ukrainian gas company that Hunter Biden joined as a board member in 2014—and debunked conspiracies that Ukraine interfered in the 2016 election. 'The evidence is overwhelming that the president abused his power by ramping up that pressure, by conditioning a wanted White House meeting and a needed military aid that had been approved in order to get that president to investigate a political rival,' he said, adding that it was also 'clear and overwhelming that in abusing that power, the president betrayed the national interest by putting his own political prospects over the security of our country.'"

For the Republicans, who have near-unanimity as well, impeachment is a deceptive trick to stop President Trump from winning an election from a party which despises him personally but cannot beat him. The purpose of this hearing as we understand it is to discuss whether President Donald J. Trump's conduct fits the definition of a high crime and misdemeanor. It does not," [Steve Castor, counsel for House Republicans] said. 'Such that the committee should consider articles of impeachment to remove the president from office and it should not. This case in many respects comes down to eight lines in a call transcript,' Castor continued, referring to the transcript of the July call between Trump and Zelenskiy. 'Let me say clearly and unequivocally that the answer to that question is 'No," Castor added, referring back to whether Trump's actions constituted high crimes and misdemeanors.

'The record in the Democrats' impeachment inquiry does not show that President Trump abused the power of his office or obstructed Congress,' he said. 'To impeach a president who 63 million people voted for over eight lines in a call transcript is baloney."

Castor went on to say that Democrats 'seek to impeach President Trump not because they have evidence of high crimes or misdemeanors but because they disagree with his policies.' This impeachment inquiry is not the organic outgrowth of serious misconduct. Democrats have been searching for a set of facts on which to impeach President Trump since his inauguration, he added. "The Democrats and Republicans disagree as to whether impeachment should even be on the House agenda. They profoundly disagree over what the impeachment focus reveals about the President and the two parties."

It is, as all debates are, all about the struggle for agenda and spin.

Both sides argue it is not a close call.

## The unjustified incredulity of Trumphaters | COMMENTARY
*By RICHARD E. VATZ*
*FOR THE BALTIMORE SUN | JUN 11, 2020 AT 10:36 AM*

Donald Trump is the "dumbest and worst president" in American history, so said Republican attorney George Conway, seeing and raising *The Washington Post's* Jennifer Rubin's evaluation of President Trump in part of the media competition to hate him the most.

I think that James Buchanan would give Mr. Trump a run for his money as the worst, and I think that calling Mr. Trump dumbest or even dumb is, well, a "lie." Neither Trump lovers nor Trump haters will endorse or enjoy this column, and since in our polarized society, the remaining readers may well constitute the null case, prepare yourself for some unpleasant and unsatisfying rhetorical truths.

The people who detest Donald Trump cannot fathom how he can simply blatantly lie with impunity, meaning he loses no Trump-lovers when he says any of, for example, the lies that *The Washington Post* Fact Checker has catalogued. For example, Mr. Trump has actually made, The Post claimed in April, over 18,000 "false or misleading claims."

Many of these are not disputable calls (although many are). Mr. Trump claims he passed the "biggest tax cut in history," and one of his most recent and ugly prevarications was that Joe Scarborough, MSNBC anchor, may be a murderer. President Trump opined on the death of Lori Klausutis, an aide to Mr. Scarborough, that it was "a very suspicious situation…I hope somebody gets to the bottom of it…there's no statute of limitations."

How, you may wonder, could any sentient being support a president who lies so consistently, or as Trump-haters might say, so constantly?

It is due to the resentment against Trump-haters' double standard of ignoring their favorite politicians' deceptions and lies and/or rhetorically dismissing them as inconsequential. Let's look at CNN's Dana Beck's recent, widely heralded, soft-as-soft-can be, follow-up free interview with Democratic presumed nominee Joe Biden. Mr. Biden claimed wildly, "at least 35,000 to 50,000" of the estimated 100,000 deaths from the coronavirus were avoidable and caused by the president's "lack of attention and ego."

Up to half the deaths from the coronavirus were caused by the president's badly motivated decision-making? Well, that certainly calls for a question from the never-interrupting reporter Ms. Bash. What did she ask him about that shocking claim: How did he come up with such a number? What policies initiated by President Trump led to such unnecessary deaths? What did Mr. Biden recommend and at what time that would have avoided so many deaths? None of these questions or any questions regarding Mr. Biden's outrageous allegation followed.

Ms. Bash's follow-up was a statement that Mr. Trump was trying to "make fun of you," that he "was trying to belittle you and made "it seem like a sign of weakness: Is it?"—she asked, referring to Mr. Biden's wearing a mask in public. Mr. Biden hit that softball out of the park, but the game is baseball, and an interviewer is not supposed to be a batting practice pitcher. There were literally no tough inquiries in the interview shown on Wolf Blitzer's "Situation Room." Mr. Blitzer was head-over-heels about the "great" interview. There were no questions from either of those two journalists about the Tara Reade controversy, which was given significant credibility in a separate interview of her by former Fox News host Megyn Kelly. There were no questions about Mr. Biden's stuttering, stammering and confusion in interviews. No questions about previous allegations that Mr. Biden plagiarized British Labor leader Neil Kinnock in 1976. There was no information about the editing of the Biden interviews. If Mr. Biden were giving more interviews, one could say whether this was an outlier, but the non-confrontational style is typical of interviews by Democratic-leaning media sources to this point.

This writer is not arguing an equivalence between the tastelessness, outright falsities and, the newest charge, lack of empathy of Mr. Trump. I have published almost a half-dozen articles regarding how sickening this president's vile style and simple dishonesty are to me. (That is why I wrote in my presidential choice in 2016.)

But if fair-minded people are wondering why Mr. Trump's supporters do not concede their negative points, it is because of the free pass his despisers give to his critics and opponents when they make up stories, repeat their lies and have demonstrable political failings that are not addressed.

This is why charges against Mr. Trump solidify his support. There was never coverage comparable to Mr. Trump's of the President Obama promises about Obamacare. There is hardly any examination of the material questions about Vice President Biden. If Trump despisers wish to ever rhetorically move large numbers of even those conservatives or undecided centrists who are open to persuasion, there has to be some equality of incredulity regarding the weaknesses of their own political principals.

*Richard E. Vatz (rvatz@towson.edu) is professor of political persuasion at Towson University and author of The Only Authentic Book of Persuasion: the Agenda-Spin Model" (LAD Custom Publishing, 2019).*

## One-Two Years into the Biden Presidency

The 2018 description, amended through 2022, of the Agenda-Spin Award of which I am the benefactor for the Eastern Communication Association was not written overwhelmingly with former Vice President and later President Joe Biden in mind, but it could have been:

The Agenda-Spin conception of rhetoric and political persuasion is an explanatory concept which makes clear the importance of the field's presence in political, perhaps especially presidential and presidential campaign persuasion. a presence which has been increasingly neglected nationwide in recent years. The method is particularly relevant in a political era wherein there is manifest ongoing competition nationally to focus or end focus on Afghanistan, Covid, illegal immigration explosion, inflation, crime in America, and confronting China.

President Biden has overseen perhaps the most consistently rhetorically unsuccessful presidency since Herbert Hoover. Biden's policies on inflation, illegal immigration, Covid, crime in America, Russia's invasion of Ukraine, Afghanistan plus his unwillingness to engage the press in regular press conferences has earned him nearly unanimous opposition among Republicans. Rhetorically and significantly, he has earned increasing opposition from a Democratic Party whose unanimity of presidential support under Republican leaders Chuck Schumer and Nancy Pelosi has been nothing short of miraculous.

Until recently.

The Biden Administration's support of the phaseout of Title 42, a Trumpian policy that prevents illegal immigration from becoming thrice as bad as the ineffectual current situation of illegal immigrants' flooding American borders. As this is being written, contrary to the Biden Administration's efforts, the policy has been extended, but previously supportive Democratic politicians, such as Sen. Chris Coons (Sen., Delaware) and others, have joined Sens. Joe Manchin (W. Va.) and Kyrsten Sinema (Ariz.) in sponsoring a 60-day delay bill.

The reluctant anti-Biden rejection among Democrats is increasing as many Democrats reject Biden support in upcoming off-year election.

From an Agenda-Spin perspective, it is striking how the president simply ignores inflation as a topic as much as possible and depicts the economy, consensually seen as leading to recession or worse, as "doing great." [Geraghty, Jim, "President Biden Wants to Ignore Inflation," *National Review*, May 2, 2022]

This book is not intended to criticize policy, except inferentially, but when presidential efforts to manipulate agenda and spin are so out of kilter with general consensus—trying to eliminate from presidential discussion Afghanistan, crime and China in addition to inflation—even when the persuader has years of media support, it has to be noted as a rhetorical failure, a profound record of rhetorical failure.

Joe Biden may be the greatest presidential rhetorical failure since Herbert Hoover and worse than President Jimmy Carter but with more resources.

Here are a couple critically important pieces from my friend, former Maryland Gov. Robert L. Ehrlich, reflecting on President Biden's manifold rhetorical and political failures:

---

I.    9 Things the Left Has Recently Done to Transform America and Destroy Our Culture *The Western Journal*

By Bob Ehrlich May 17, 2022 at 3:21pm

Progressive Democrats have made no secret of their intent to transform a "racist" America.

That these woke activists seek to do so by devaluing American culture issue by issue, step by step is quite clear. Think about it:

**OCCUPY WALL STREET**

The establishment of filthy tent city encampments around the centerpiece of American capitalism was short-lived. Yet what most of us saw as a rather pitiful attempt to devalue (embarrass) American commerce gave rise to today's woke socialists.

It also marked the escalation of an intimidation campaign against big business that has enjoyed considerable success. As a result, a large component of corporate America willingly falls for any lefty cause that comes down the pike.

Interestingly, long gone are the days when the Hillary Clintons of the world would fire up campaign crowds by demonizing big businesses' win in Citizens United. In this case, the "enemy" simply folded its hand.

## DEFUND THE POLICE

This beauty was an attempt to devalue law and order by taking money and therefore personnel away from the very people tasked with defending us. Clearly ludicrous from the jump, it nevertheless had considerable impact on the rhetoric and voting behavior of many Democrats over the past 18 months.

But all terrible ideas must come to an end. This one has lost steam as so many of America's most beautiful cities (Seattle, San Francisco, Portland, Chicago) have descended into chaos.

## OPEN BORDERS

What better way to denigrate and ruin a country than to devalue the people who protect its national borders? Recall the widely reported allegation that Border Patrol agents on horseback had whipped illegal migrants. Open borders advocates (and their sponsors in Congress) took full political advantage, until video evidence revealed the allegations to be patently false.

As usual, no apologies were forthcoming. Still, a nonstop campaign to emasculate our Border Patrol continues unabated.

## COVID-19

No pandemic-era mission was more important to the new left than the (generally successful) campaign to close churches, synagogues and mosques… while keeping liquor stores open.

Here, a secularized left was able to devalue religious observance by reducing religious practice to just another mundane activity subject to government control. You might rightly interpret these events as yet another chapter in the left's relentless campaign to degrade religious freedom.

## CONGRESS AND THE COURTS

The most direct way to devalue American institutions is to change the rules that govern them.

Hence, the public is force-fed demands to eliminate the Electoral College (whenever Democrats lose presidential races) or do away with the Senate filibuster (only a racist tactic when employed by Republicans) or pack the Supreme Court (again, whenever Democrats are on the losing end of a 5-4 or 6-3 court decision). All in all, a transparently unsuccessful tactic to date.

## CIVIL DISOBEDIENCE

One way to devalue dissent within civil society is unhinged disobedience whenever things don't go your way.

The progressive media may rationalize such actions as "mostly peaceful," but the vast majority of Americans recognize riots, looting, fires and the wholesale destruction of property for what they are. Note that intimidation tactics utilized against public officials (which are by definition illegal) count here as well.

## SPEECH AND DISSENT: PART I

The relatively recent campaign to debase speech through Big Tech/big government control took a massive hit with the revelation that Hunter Biden's infamous laptop is not Russian disinformation but indeed real. This was followed by a second significant hit when news broke of a quietly assembled group (the "Disinformation Bureau") within an agency (the Department of Homeland Security) that has utterly failed to perform its central mission of protecting the border.

But do not miss the central point: Both moves constitute direct attempts to devalue First Amendment rights.

## SPEECH AND DISSENT: PART II

The proliferation of speech codes, trigger warnings and safe spaces across the college landscape is an unfortunate matter of fact.

But these invented constructs are no accident. The indoctrination of young people into devaluing their own liberty had to start somewhere. And what better place than our genuinely woke and uber-expensive echo chambers, better known as American colleges and universities?

## SPEECH AND DISSENT: PART III

An unforeseen but beneficial byproduct of pandemic-related education shutdowns has been the outing of inappropriate progressive material in our high schools, middle schools and even elementary schools. As a result, the campaign to devalue parental rights in the classroom began to take on water in Virginia last fall. It took on a lot more water in Texas just last week.

Fortunately, it appears that no amount of backtracking or cover-ups or cries of racism will cool off a parent power movement growing from coast to coast.

Concluding thought: All manmade things are a work in progress, and America is no exception. But deliberate attempts to devalue our basic institutions are a path toward mediocrity, and worse.

Robert Ehrlich is a former governor of Maryland as well as a former U.S. congressman and state legislator. He is the author of "Bet You Didn't See That One Coming: Obama, Trump, and the End of Washington's Regular Order," in addition to "Turn This Car Around," "America: Hope for Change" and "Turning Point." Ehrlich is currently a counsel at the firm of King & Spalding in Washington, D.C.

**II.** Ehrlich: Now That They See Biden in Power, the 'Gruesome Foursome' Will Come A-Knocking

**By Bob Ehrlich March 8, 2022 at 5:29pm** *The Western Journal*

"[The invasion of Ukraine] could have a profound negative impact on the climate….I hope President Putin will help us to stay on track with respect to what we need to do for the climate."—climate czar John Kerry (the same John Kerry who had James Taylor sing to the French people in the aftermath of the Charlie Hebdo terror attack)

"The war in Afghanistan is now over. …When I was running for president, I made a commitment to the American people that I would end this war. Today I have honored that commitment."—President Joe Biden after America's humiliating withdrawal from Afghanistan

"I haven't been to Europe. I don't understand the point you're making."—Vice President Kamala Harris in answer to the question of why the person in charge of the southern border had not bothered to visit the southern border.

"Most of the economic problems we're facing (inflation, supply chains, etc.) are high class problems."—Jason Furnan, former Obama economist, in a tweet endorsed by Biden chief of staff Ron Klain

The foregoing statements were made by people in positions of power. Note that none of these statements was a faux pas, a mistake quickly corrected. Indeed, all were delivered as intended for wide consumption and should remain recorded for posterity.

The first word that comes to (the reasonable) mind is "unserious," an indictment born of our Biden-era transformation into a weak and woke culture. It is an opinion widely held by average Americans, as poll after poll reflects growing disdain for progressive policy.

But the audience is not simply the American people. The world's despots are watching as well. And they are no doubt encouraged by what they see.

The murderous lineup is familiar: Vladimir Putin in Russia, Xi Jinping in China, Khamenei in Iran, Kim Jong Un in North Korea. This gruesome foursome is always probing, always looking for ways to exploit cracks in what they regard as the American façade.

Today they see a downsized, woke military whose leadership is all-in on hunting down white supremacists and attempting to convince the public that the greatest threat to the world is climate change. They see an administration intent on negotiating away America's natural resource advantage. They see an embarrassing, irresponsible withdrawal from Afghanistan. They see a president determined to placate a notorious sponsor of terror in Tehran.

Above all, they see a declining superpower beset with internal strife and going about the business of questioning its own cultural values.

And so Putin invades a sovereign Ukraine after successful adventures in Chechnya, Georgia and Crimea. Xi regularly sends fighter jets into Taiwanese airspace. The mullahs supersize their ballistic missile program while pursuing a pathway to nuclear status. And can you imagine Kim's take on all of this?

Sudden thought: Wasn't the last election supposed to be about putting the "adults" back in charge?

Being unserious during times of peace and prosperity carries a price. Think about the attempts to exclude parents from their children's education, or the idea that boys should be allowed to compete in girls' athletics, or the race-obsessed notion that babies are born either oppressors or oppressed. But even these initiatives do not place the country in immediate peril.

Being unserious in wartime is different. It encourages troublemakers to push the envelope—and in the process makes the world a far more dangerous place.

The free world benefits when America is serious. The free world breathes easier when the bad guys are fearful of American power, and especially American presidents.

Here's hoping a sense of order—of seriousness—can be restored in November.

Robert Ehrlich is a former governor of Maryland as well as a former U.S. congressman and state legislator. He is the author of "Bet You Didn't See That One Coming: Obama, Trump, and the End of Washington's Regular Order," in addition to "Turn This Car Around," "America: Hope for Change" and "Turning Point." Ehrlich is currently a counsel at the firm of King & Spalding in Washington, D.C.

---

## The Agenda-Spin Method and the 2024 Presidential Election

Throughout this book I have argued that all persuasion is effected through the winning of the struggle for agenda and spin, and the presidential election of 2024 is no exception; in fact, it is a perfect example.

Again, simplified, the Agenda-Spin Method constitutes examining the fight for what matters become salient to audiences and what those matters mean.

The 2024 presidential election was from the beginning a battle over what to talk about and the significance of said agendas and spins.

The issue of the president's age and ability to function as president festered and festered with minimal coverage by the main networks of ABC, CBS and NBC until finally Biden was forced to step down pursuant to his disastrous debate with former president Donald Trump wherein he (Biden) lost his train of thought, and supporters like CNN's said pursuant to the debate that he had had a "shaky" debate.

https://www.cnn.com/politics/live-news/presidential-debate-biden-trump-06-28-24/index.html

The reaction to Biden's performance grew so indisputable that he withdrew from the race and was replaced by Kamala Harris amid rumors of resentment by the Biden campaign and Jill Biden.

Through the election, rumors of Biden's neurological inability hung in the background and served as a source of questions surrounding the Democratic party's cohesiveness.

Ultimately a major exposé was written in The Wall Street Journal, revealing how the White House tried to protect the mentally incapable Biden from having to deal with difficult matters such as the precipitous withdrawal from Afghanistan and chronic matters like his early fatigue and brain fog which occurred periodically.

https://www.wsj.com/politics/biden-white-house-age-function-diminished-3906a839?mod=Searchresults_pos7&page=1

In the weeks leading up to the campaign, the unavailability of Vice President Harris to meet with the press or to actively campaign made some pundits incredulous, yet as election day approached, she was projected to be the odds-on winner.

An article this author wrote for The Baltimore Post-Examiner which references my Facebook prognostication, initially made weeks before the election and reiterated the morning of the election before any results were known, makes this clear (and keep in mind that the average of polls showed Harris winning the popular vote (https://projects.fivethirtyeight.com/polls/president-general/2024/national/) and the electoral vote (https://projects.fivethirtyeight.com/2024-election-forecast/)...

I knew and wrote early on (June 20, 2024) that Vice President Kamala Harris would be a devastatingly bad Democratic choice as presidential nominee: "The greatest current fear is that Joe might have to yield his 2nd four years of presidency to Vice President Kamala Harris, who is distinguished by having less support than the president."

https://lapostexaminer.com/hope-for-democratic-optimism-in-the-2024-presidential-election-from-a-conservative/2024/06/20

Here without editing is my Facebook post the morning of the election, November 5, 2024, before I knew of any votes:

---

## For Election Outcomes, Listen to Those in Political Rhetoric
November 6, 2024 Richard E. Vatz, Ph.D

I had read all of the overconfident prognosticators who predicted Kamala's victory (accent on the first syllable, Harris Haters), and I smiled.

Here without editing is my Facebook post the morning of the election, before I knew of any votes:

### Election Proclamation: Trump Will Win and No One Will Be Able to Explain to Me My One Surprise

Doubling Down on My Prediction: As I wrote previously on my Facebook page and have said recently on a variety of media, I think Trump will win. I think it is like 1980 when people had serious doubts about Ronald Reagan but didn't, as Americans, want to throw up their hands and wimpily say "We cannot do better than Carter has done for the last 4 years."

Win or lose, Kamala has run the dumbest political and rhetorical campaign I have ever witnessed...as I said on WBFF [station in Baltimore] this a.m., you don't refuse an audience with Joe Rogan, you don't refuse to say publicly how you voted on Prop 36 designed to make multiple shoplifting a felony and increase penalties for fentanyl commerce, miss the Correspondents' Dinner, and call your opponent a fascist.

I am not unsophisticated in politics, having taught political persuasion for over 1/2 a century; the only thing that has surprised me—the \only\ thing—in this election campaign is Harrison Ford's endorsement of Kamala Harris.

None of this means that I am incapable of error.

---

All of those who say they have virtually never been wrong—[Allan Lichtman, are you listening—how are things today? As The Guardian printed, "Allan Lichtman had correctly forecast the result of nine of the past 10 US presidential elections (and even the one he didn't, in 2000, he insists was stolen from Al

Gore).—His predictions were based on rational decision-making criteria, inferior to basing predictions on the ability to control the agenda and spin.]

https://www.theguardian.com/us-news/2024/nov/16/trump-election-forecast-allan-lichtman

My prediction—rarely do I make predictions and almost never with certitude—was based on 50 years of examining elections and rarely making predictions. There are multiple lessons for the Democrats, some few of which are in my post, but the most important one is this: nominate people who are good and wise at running the government and who are not noxious to a near-majority of the country.

The reason Harris never answered material questions is that there are no responses that address irresponsible political decisions: ignoring the illegal migrant invasion, not supporting more strongly Israel, our singular Middle East major [democratic] ally, spending the United States into penury (take note as well, Mr. Trump) and ignoring crime and public safety on the streets.

There is of course extensive schadenfreude, which Democrats should take with good grace.

As I have stated repeatedly and written, Donald Trump is a repellent personality, but Americans will support a candidate—I did—when the alternative and her party are so bereft of good judgment.

https://baltimorepostexaminer.com/for-election-outcomes-listen-to-those-in-political-rhetoric/2024/11/06

---

Kamala Harris lost because she violated all of the conventions of agenda-spin and rhetorical commonplaces: control and address the issues that people find reasonable; control the interpretation of what those issues should mean to people; and be publicly available.

There are issues that are employable in elections. In this one they included the illegal migrant invasion, unmitigated by the calling of such illegals "undocumented migrants;" the inflation that inhabited the country at the beginning of the Biden Administration; climate change (made difficult by the colder weather that hit America by November); tough posture toward Russia vis-a-vis Middle East and China regarding Ukraine and Taiwan; support of Israel; personal likeability of a candidate, etc.

Harris and her supporters tried to minimize the crisis of illegals and occasional murders of innocents such as Laken Riley, Jocelyn Nungary and others.

https://www.dailysignal.com/2024/07/06/13-lives-lost-hands-illegal-aliens-past-12-months/

Moreover, the Harris team avoided press conferences and consistently tried to make the issue of the campaign the specter of Donald Trump's becoming president.

This writer, who had never voted for Trump, voted reluctantly for him for the first time due to the ignoring of the border issue, the misinterpretation of inflation as transitory and the soft support of Israel and the very salient ignoring of Israeli Prime Minister Benjamin Netanyahu by the Harris-Tim Walz ticket when he spoke to the U.S. Congress. The Biden-Harris fecklessness regarding China was another disturbing perception of many who opposed Harris.

The election outcome surprised Harris, to say the least, leading her to delay calling President-elect Trump to congratulate him, but it didn't amaze those of us who wondered all along why she was unavailable for press questioning and how she could imply by lack of word and deed that she thought the migrant invasion and inflation was little ado about nothing.

But CNN described Harris' campaign's reaction to the loss of the presidency as full of "shock and disbelief."

https://www.cnn.com/2024/11/06/politics/video/kamala-harris-campaign-reaction-election-trump-digvid

They needed to pay more attention to the agenda on which they focused and the spin they attached to it.

THUS CONCLUDES THE LESSONS of *The Only Authentic Book of Persuasion*. The message of this book, stated and restated throughout, is that persuasion is the struggle to create agenda and spin for chosen audiences.

Throughout the history of the debate on the relationship between rhetoric and situations, much has been written; in my opinion, much of that which has been written on behalf of the situational perspective is academically mystifying, irrelevant, anti-persuasion, non-persuasive, and simply wrong-headed. The perspective that situations dictate rhetoric makes the fields of communication studies and rhetoric embarrassingly subordinate to fields that successfully claim to be able to explain better what the "real situation" is, fields such as politics (I'm sorry—political science, which is a "science" because that is the meaning infused by the persuaders of that field), history, and a multitude of other disciplines. Parenthetically, one of my best all-time colleagues is Jack Fruchtman of Towson University's Political Science Department. I am not against political inquiry, of course; I am only against rhetorically spinning it as a science.

Persuasion is involved in almost all, but not all, endeavors of human communication; e.g., debate (What is the topic? What does specific evidence mean? Who won?); interpersonal communication (Who determines about what we speak? Who may participate? What is accepted as evidence?); speeches, of course (What is the topic? Who may speak? What is accepted as evidence?); political contests; labeling behavior (brave, sick, courageous, foolhardy, etc.); the courtroom (What is allowed to be said? Who is allowed to testify? What evidence is acceptable? and What is unacceptable?); and all human discourse aimed at influencing others.

Logic really has little relevance to persuasion, as it merely tells you rules that may or may not be followed, and they have nothing to do with effectiveness of persuasion; in fact, logical fallacies are just names persuasively given to arguments we choose to reject. Oh, is that a "glittering generality?" How about this little generality, glittering or not, from a persuasion text referenced herein: "[Philosophers] cannot persuade people to make ethical judgments …?" Informal logical fallacies are unacceptable in others' communications and acceptable in our own-consistently.

Persuasion is one of the most exciting subjects of discourse, but it is rarely determined by situations; it is determined by human agents and human agency: who decides what is the subject at hand, what it means, and what should be done about it.

Arbitrarily defining an unheard sound as no sound at all.

The author wrote a few words about the end of the Trump presidency and the beginning of President Biden's with at least two years impending of Democratic control of the House and Senate.

The 2020 election campaign, as with all political campaigns, was a struggle for agenda and spin, but more stark and polarized than perhaps any other. I have been assigned to write a chapter about this in a book on presidential campaigns, coming out, I believe, in 2022.

Let me just summarize that the entire four years of the Trump presidency comprised agenda issues emphasized and/or ignored by partisan media and spin in diametric opposition. As my letter title two years ago in *The Washington Post* summed it up, "It's impossible to find a disinterested view of this presidency." https://www.washingtonpost.com/opinions/its-impossible-to-find-a-disinterested-view-of-this-presidency/2018/08/02/0aa61cf6-94ef-11e8-818b-e9b7348cd87d_story.html.

In such an atmosphere, the value of reluctant testimony becomes paramount: when Republicans like Atty. Gen. Bill Barr, Sen. Lindsey Graham, and Education Secretary Betsy DeVos resolutely opposed President Trump's behavior in the last days of his election persuasion and the attack on the Capitol, it is highly persuasive. Indeed, it led to the president's conceding the election and strongly condemning the violence.

If you want to read an exemplary quote of some genuinely reluctant testimony, take Mr. Barr's: "Orchestrating a mob to pressure Congress is inexcusable. The president's conduct yesterday was a betrayal of his office and supporters."

President Trump addressed followers in Georgia before the Senatorial run-off, emphasizing his election reversal attempts and only secondarily his support for the Republican run-off candidates. The day before the rioting, he told his legion of followers, "You will never take back our country with weakness."

I wrote on my Facebook page:

CRIMINAL OUTRAGE

--------------------------

The despicable miscreants who are attacking the Capitol must be stopped, caught and prosecuted. Mr. President...go on national television and demand they stop and be stopped. This is not an ambiguous situation...act as a president...now.

------------------------------

Update…president just spoke, emphasizing that the election was stolen, and then he told protesters to go home…complaining that others will use their actions against the correctly outraged Trump supporters…

NO! Wrong timing, wrong emphasis, wrong vehicle, a late, taped audio message, followed by a video of 1 minute. No recognition of the appalling nature of the act. This was your opportunity to say "There is no excuse for such an attack, and the perpetrators must be stopped and incarcerated."

You blew it, Mr. President, and the country and your supporters will suffer. When people look back on your presidency, most will remember "Opportunity Lost."

------------------------------

*Sometimes choices in agenda and spin are temporary; sometimes they last for decades and more.*

*~Vatz*

------------------------------

Whereas all leaders are in the consistent Agenda-Spin struggle for persuasion of national and international audiences as well as the United States electorate within the former, there has rarely been such a consistent disconnect between liberals and conservatives. The Agenda-Spin fight will dominate all future elections more than it has even in past elections and always will be the currency for all persuasion.

# Addendum

❖

Post sent to the Communication Research and Theory Network of the National Communication Association, May 30, 2019

## Agenda-Spin and the Mueller Speech

Colleagues: what a valuable rhetorical/persuasive analysis per the Agenda-Spin model you can provide in papers or on electronic media, per Special counsel's Robert S. Mueller live televised remarks yesterday at the Justice Department. (I shall be providing my interpretation on 50,000 watts in Baltimore Saturday Night.)

Why was he speaking? He said he would not go beyond the 448-page report he provided weeks ago, and in his short speech he didn't. Or did he?

Was the speech responsible or irresponsible? Was he sending a message, and was that his charge? What was the message? He took no questions: Wise? Dereliction of duty? Was he steady or unsure of himself?

Hillary Clinton supporter and Harvard Professor of Law Emeritus Alan Dershowitz reluctantly testified in *The Hill* (or was it not reluctant testimony?), "No prosecutor should ever say or do anything for the purpose of helping one party or the other. I cannot imagine a plausible reason why Mueller went beyond his report and gratuitously suggested that President Trump might be guilty, except to help Democrats in Congress and to encourage impeachment talk and action. Shame on Mueller for abusing his position of trust and for allowing himself to be used for such partisan advantage."

Former U.S. Attorney Joseph diGenova argued on radio that Mueller was contemptibly irresponsible and that "…he fell back on the convoluted language in his report, hoping to obfuscate an issue that Attorney General William Barr had previously clarified by determining that the special counsel's investigation did not produce sufficient evidence to justify charging President Trump with obstructing justice. 'If we had had confidence that the president clearly did not commit a crime, we would have said so,' Mueller told reporters, explaining that, as part of the Justice Department, his office was 'bound by' the OLC's opinion. 'Charging the president with a crime was, therefore, not an option we could consider,' Mueller said…

If President Trump actually committed a crime, there is nothing in the OLC's opinion that would have prevented the special counsel or the attorney general from saying so.

Sen. Kirsten Gillibrand, on the other hand, saw the speech as a clear message to Congress to impeach, tweeting that "the White House has repeatedly stonewalled Congress' ability to take basic fact-finding steps. [That,] combined with Mueller's clear message today, tells me that Republicans and Democrats should begin impeachment hearings."

*The New York Times* wrote that Julian Epstein, counsel to the Democrats in the Clinton impeachment, as well as some Fox principals, thought that "the special counsel effectively refuted Mr. Trump's no-collusion, no-obstruction mantra. While repeating that he found no illegal coordination between Mr. Trump and Russia, Mr. Mueller clearly left the impression that he saw serious wrongdoing by the president in his attempts to thwart the investigation."

Journalist Barbara McQuade's title in today's *The Daily Beast* says it all for her, "Mueller's Seething Message: This Isn't a Hoax, This Is a Crime: The special counsel is too reserved to say what he really means: Russia attacked America and Trump broke the law."

It's all about Agenda-Spin, and those in our field should have as much to say about the Mueller speech as anyone.

www.ingramcontent.com/pod-product-compliance
Lightning Source LLC
Chambersburg PA
CBHW080421030426
42335CB00020B/2538